Challenging behaviours in mainstream schools

Practical strategies
for effective intervention
and reintegration

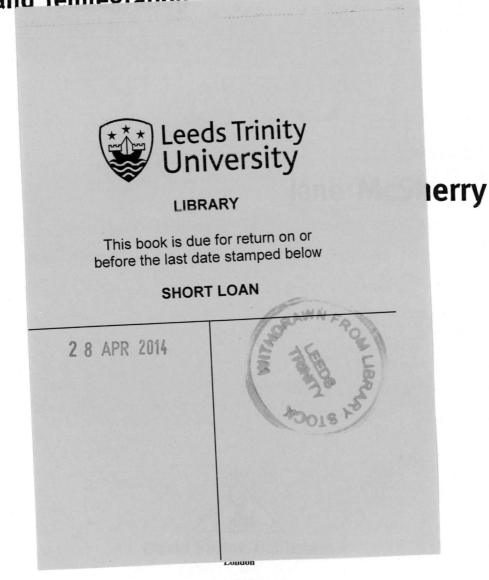

erry

London

David Fulton Publishers
2 Park Square, Milton Park, Abingdon, Oxon OX14 4RN

270 Madison Avenue, New York, NY 10016

First published in Great Britain in 2001 by David Fulton Publishers
Transferred to digital printing

David Fulton Publishers is an imprint of the Taylor & Francis Group, an informa business

British Library Cataloguing in Publication Data
A catalogue record for this book is available from the British Library.

ISBN 1-85346-746-4

Typeset by FiSH Books, London

Contents

For David, Callum and Morag

Acknowledgements

Thanks are due to Doug Bone and the staff and pupils of Wandle Valley School where the inspiration for the original programme developed; also to all the staff and pupils in Wandsworth schools who have so enthusiastically worked with the programme.

Special thanks go the Inclusion Project team who have disseminated the programme so effectively in schools.

A debt of gratitude is owed to colleagues who read the manuscript and offered thoughtful insights from their professional expertise: Sue Clarke, Professor Duncan Harris, Trevor Harper, Sonia Hulejczuk and Trish Press.

Also, the help of colleagues who prepared case studies is acknowledged: Andy Hough (Francis Barber Pupil Referral Unit) and Gordon Middleton (Granard Primary Learning Support Unit).

Introduction

Questions the Introduction aims to answer
What is this book about?
How is this book structured and how can I effectively use it?

Dealing with children with EBD (emotional and behavioural difficulties) may be seen as an intractable and frustrating task for teachers. The difficulties are genuine. But EBD is often engendered or worsened by the environment, including schools' or teachers' responses. Schools have a significant effect on children's behaviour, and vary widely in the extent to which they help children overcome their difficulties.   (DfEE 1994b)

The same statements could be applied to pupils with challenging behaviours who can exhibit social, emotional and behavioural difficulties (or any combination of these elements). Pupils who are disaffected also fall within the umbrella of challenging behaviour. The term 'challenging behaviours' has a more positive emphasis as it prompts us as teachers and professionals working with the pupils to 'rise to the challenge' rather than see the problems as lying within the pupil. O'Brien (1998) has summarised another positive aspect of the term 'challenging behaviour':

The term is open to whole-school definition, and thus can also be identified in school policy as behaviour that requires extra support from the school management team.   (O'Brien 1998)

Both terms have been used in this book (emotional and behavioural difficulties and challenging behaviours), as they seemed appropriate for that section or point. A pupil who is exhibiting challenging behaviour is undoubtedly finding that this leads to social, emotional and behavioural problems or difficulties for them at that time. Equally pupils 'diagnosed' as having emotional and behavioural difficulties are generally presenting challenging behaviours to those around them. This book offers strategies for working with pupils whose behaviour is seen as challenging in whatever form.

This book has developed from the author's work with pupils with emotional and behavioural difficulties; with their teachers who have demonstrated a real desire to work with these pupils; with schools striving to implement inclusive policies for pupils with challenging behaviour, and with LEAs proactively attempting to aid schools in this work.

Intended logical progress of book

The book describes a continuum of educational provision for pupils with challenging behaviour in mainstream schools and pupil referral units. The same approach has been successfully used in a special school setting for re-integrating pupils with emotional and behavioural difficulties into mainstream schools. The book is structured in a progressive way, starting with the core elements of the programme (Part One, Chapters 1 to 4) and progressing through the various applications of the programme (Part Two, Chapters 5 to 9).

Part One: Core elements of the programme

Chapter 1 sets the context for the model on which the programme is based; this explains the core ideas that underlie the work. These ideas will be developed and built upon in subsequent chapters. Chapter 2 explains the original programme's conception and development. The original programme was devised and used in an all age special school for pupils with emotional and behavioural difficulties. The programme has three parts: assessment, preparation and support. The assessment tool developed was called the Re-integration Readiness Scale (RRS) (McSherry 1996). Chapter 3 explains how the original programme (for use in a special school for pupils with emotional and behavioural difficulties) was used and developed for mainstream use. The Coping in Schools Scale (CISS) is the mainstream version of the Re-integration Readiness Scale. Chapter 3 also explains how information collected using the CISS can be used. It provides additional insight into areas of strength and weakness and assists in developing possible strategies for intervention and support. Chapter 4 explores the group work approach (used as the second key part of the programme), why it works the way it does and how it can be applied throughout the continuum for pupils with challenging behaviour and/or emotional and behavioural difficulties (Figure 1). This group work approach forms part of the approach used at all stages of the continuum.

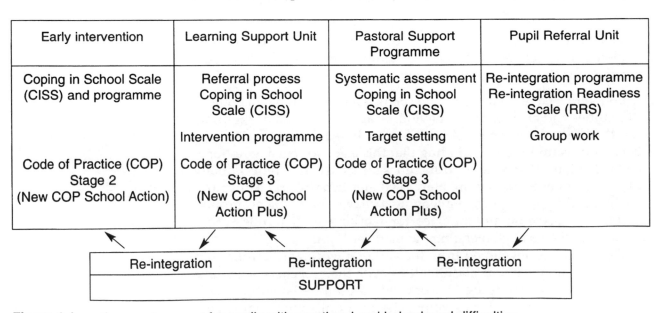

Early intervention	Learning Support Unit	Pastoral Support Programme	Pupil Referral Unit
Coping in School Scale (CISS) and programme	Referral process Coping in School Scale (CISS)	Systematic assessment Coping in School Scale (CISS)	Re-integration programme Re-integration Readiness Scale (RRS)
	Intervention programme	Target setting	Group work
Code of Practice (COP) Stage 2 (New COP School Action)	Code of Practice (COP) Stage 3 (New COP School Action Plus)	Code of Practice (COP) Stage 3 (New COP School Action Plus)	

Re-integration	Re-integration	Re-integration
SUPPORT		

Figure 1 A continuum of support for pupils with emotional and behavioural difficulties

Part Two: Applications of the programme

The following chapters then move us through the continuum, starting with early intervention (Chapter 5) using the example of primary/ secondary transfer work for pupils who are at risk because of their emotional and behavioural difficulties. The application of the programme in Learning Support Units (Chapter 6) is based upon both research on in-school centres and the author's experience of supporting the establishment of LSUs across one Local Education Authority. The next stage on the continuum is Pastoral Support Programmes for pupils in danger of permanent exclusion (Chapter 7). Chapter 8 discusses the off-site element of the continuum model and looks at re-integration of pupils from Pupil Referral Units, reflecting on good practice in this area. Chapter 9 draws key elements of the continuum together and briefly suggests further possible applications of the programme.

How to use this book

This book can be used in a number of ways. I hope I have written a book that will be readable in a traditional sense – from beginning to end. Reading it this way will give you a feel for the progression of an original idea into a workable and adaptable programme. It will offer an insight into the role that my colleagues have played in extending the process. It is important to stress that the programme is adaptable and can be used in a variety of ways while still offering a basic structure and continuity within an institution or across institutions. It has been my intention to illustrate the adaptability of the programme and readers are urged to be creative in their application of it. The process can be applied to both primary and secondary pupils and I have tried to use illustrations from both phases where possible.

The book could also be used for reference purposes relating to a specific area, for example, Learning Support Units with linked schools (pages 66–9) or questions to consider when preparing re-integration for pupils from a Pupil Referral Unit (Appendix 9).

Outlined below are possible ways that the book can be used by teachers, Learning Support Unit managers, re-integration coordinators and LEA advisers.

For those short on time

For everyone, Chapters 1 and 2 are the best place to start, as they give an overview of the context of the programme and how it was developed.

The panel below indicates the key chapters to read (depending on your role) if you do not have time to read through the book in a linear progression.

Role	Chapters to read
Classroom teacher	1 to 4
LSU manager	1 to 4, 6
SENCO	1 to 4, 6, 7
Anyone concerned with Year 6/7 transfer	1 to 5
Key professionals concerned with PRU re-integration	1 to 4, 8
LEA advisers on inclusion	1 to 9

Structure of the chapters

- Questions the chapter will attempt to answer.
- Detailed development and discussion of ideas using case studies (as appropriate).
- Key points.
- Food for thought.

Questions

Each chapter starts with a list of questions that the chapter aims to answer. These are designed to assist the reader by clarifying the aims of the chapter.

Development and discussion of ideas and use of case studies

In each chapter ideas and strategies are developed and discussed. Where appropriate these are illustrated by the use of case studies. The case studies either illustrate a particular way of applying the programme or the importance of specific strategies for successful inclusion.

Key points

The main section of each chapter ends with a summary of key points that will pull together the ideas that have been presented into a brief format.

Food for thought

At the end of each chapter is a section offering 'food for thought' on wider issues around inclusion which reflect issues raised in the main body of the chapter. These are linked to a set of questions. These questions have been designed to promote discussion in staff groups, or provide INSET group activities, dealing with these wider related issues. The aim is to provide staff with a framework for self-reflection and development of good practice in working with pupils with challenging behaviour.

Key points

- ➤ This book can be used in a number of ways.
- ➤ Each chapter starts with questions that the chapter aims to answer and the main section ends with a summary of key points. These are to enable you to use the book more effectively.
- ➤ A food-for-thought section at the end of each chapter presents wider issues, which reflect those raised in the main body of the chapter.

Food for thought

Once the term 'behaviour' appears in a label associated with a child it usually does not need to be followed by the word 'difficulty'. Used on its own, the assumption will be that we are about to talk of violent, dangerous, anti-social, disruptive or 'naughty' behaviour. It does not imply that we are about to talk of the positive attributes of the child or young person. It also gives no indication that we will be recognising what the child *can* do.

(O'Brien 1998)

Questions

Either with colleagues or on your own, reflecting on a pupil you work with whom you see as either having social, emotional and behavioural difficulties or challenging behaviour, think about the following questions:

Which of the terms did you choose to describe the pupil and why?

Do you think the term you chose makes a difference to how you see this pupil?

You may have immediately thought of the 'problems' this pupil has. What are the positive things that this pupil can do?

Does thinking about the positive make a difference to how you might approach working with this pupil?

Part One

Core elements of the programme

Chapter 1

The underlying framework

Questions this chapter aims to answer
What is the context of the approach presented?
What are the key elements of the approach?
How might it be used in schools and across an LEA?

Context of the approach

In the inclusion approach that this book will explain and illustrate there are some key themes that the reader will see recurring and which underpin the author's work with pupils. The approach uses a framework which can be utilised at varying stages of the continuum (see Figure 1, page 2). The framework is the Coping in Schools programme, which will be explained in detail in subsequent chapters. This framework focuses on teacher–pupil interactions and works towards cognitive behavioural change to improve those interactions. We are not only aiming to change the behaviour of pupils and their teachers within these interactions but also to change the way the behaviour and its consequence are viewed or thought about. This cognitive change is enhanced by the application of a transactional model where interactions are seen within the context of previous encounters between teacher and pupil and their influence on the present encounter. These central encounters are also put within the context of wider transactions involving peers, family, social environment and school environment. Having acknowledged the importance of these wider influences on the central transactions (between teacher and pupil) it is vital that we harness all the support available for any cognitive change. Involving and working with parents will be a recurrent theme.

Any approach to inclusion is most effectively applied as part of a whole-school strategy or approach. The application of a model across the schools in a specific area or across an LEA will further enhance the approach.

Each of the main areas encompassed in the context of the inclusion approach will be explored briefly below.

- Previous experiences and their effect on the here and now: a transactional model.
- Teacher–pupil interactions: working towards cognitive change.
- Involving and working with parents/carers.
- A whole-school approach.
- A whole LEA approach.

Previous experiences and their effect on the here and now: a transactional model

When we deal with pupils, especially pupils with emotional and behavioural difficulties, we need to see each interaction as part of a wider pattern of events within which they are involved. The pupil has a large and complex world around them (as do we as adults) and school may or may not feature as a very important part of that life. We also bring to each interaction or transaction experiences from previous encounters and these experiences inform and influence subsequent encounters.

Previous experiences and interactions inform all transactions between the pupil and peers and adults. The pupil who arrives angry because of an argument at home and consequently copes less well with his or her new maths teacher influences all subsequent interactions with this teacher. If the teacher responds in a positive and supportive way this too will influence subsequent meetings. A negative and bullying response on the part of the teacher will also influence future transactions, although obviously in a different way. This idea is presented diagrammatically in Figure 1.1.

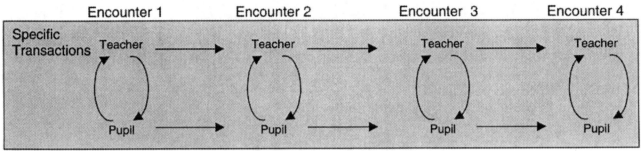

Figure 1.1 Simple transactional model (Adapted from Sameroff 1987)

If this series of transactions is increasingly negative it is important to break the cycle of negativity and begin a fresh set of transactions. In terms of applying a process for change where situations are not working, both parties need to change and work on specific targets. Pupils who exhibit challenging behaviours in school present problems for:

• the management of the school;
• themselves;
• peers;
• parents.

Conversely, all these elements present problems for the pupil. Equally, the school and their child's peer group may be presenting problems for parents. The solution lies in an approach that looks at the contributing factors brought by all to the situation. In the transactional model illustrated below in Figure 1.2 it is clear that the multiple transactions influence each subsequent transaction and all need to participate in the solution.

As professionals working with the pupil we are in the best position to take a responsible lead and attempt to break the cycle. It may not be easy as habits are difficult to break and the child will have to be

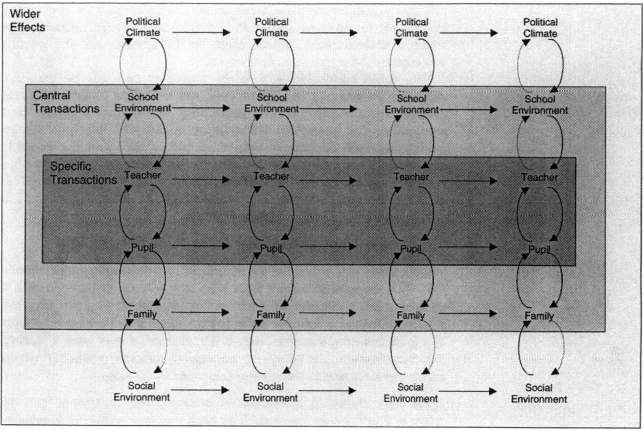

Figure 1.2 More complex transactional model

convinced that a new transactional pattern is being established. It may be additionally challenging if the child is trying hard not to let anyone get too close at that moment.

We are looking for a change in the way that various participants view the process: a cognitive change to help break negative cycles that have developed. For example, as the teacher you may see this pupil as challenging to teach because he or she interrupts your lesson by shouting out and irritates other pupils by taking their belongings. If we shift the focus for a moment, suppose that the pupil interrupts because he or she is not able to concentrate and therefore keeps losing the thread of the lesson. Maybe the pupil is late for the beginning of the lesson and misses the introduction. By shouting out he or she slows the process down and is able to follow and maybe have some control over the rest of the lesson. Maybe the pupil takes other pupils' belongings because he or she has lost or mislaid their own or never had them in the first place. Just by stopping to consider the possible, if not plausible, explanations we have inevitably shifted the focus from feeling personally affronted by the behaviour to seeing it in the context of some need that this pupil may have. Just by stopping to consider these things it changes our response because it has changed the way we are thinking about

Teacher–pupil interactions: working towards cognitive change

this pupil. It does not necessarily mean the behaviours will go away but it may change our response and this may in turn influence the cycle of transactions, which might in turn influence the pupil's subsequent behaviours in this lesson.

The pupil may receive a fairly negative and maybe punitive response for interrupting the teacher and irritating other pupils. He or she may interpret this as indicating the teacher's dislike and respond to this perceived information negatively. If pupils can be given time and support to reflect on behaviours and the possible responses, they may also be able to re-interpret other people's responses in the light of this information.

Case Study 1.1

A re-integration group at the Pupil Referral Unit

While working with a group of secondary pupils preparing to transfer from a PRU to a mainstream school we looked at the issue of trying to view a situation from a different perspective. We completed a group exercise, involving role-play, asking the pupils to think about their possible responses to a pupil behaving inappropriately in a classroom if they were a teacher. This behaviour involved being non-cooperative, swearing and being verbally abusive when asked to comply with basic classroom rules.

Some very interesting conversations followed, with comments from the pupils in their roles as teachers. They felt it was impossible not to respond to this deliberate provocation, especially as the teacher had the rest of the class to think about. They all followed a very punitive model and would take no nonsense! When we approached the issue of taking a more understanding view they seriously discussed all the problems associated with being too lenient and a very effective discussion took place.

They were then asked to reflect on their own behaviour in the past and how teachers had responded. The pupils themselves reflected that it was interesting to think about the classroom from a different perspective and that this was a valuable lesson for all pupils and teachers at regular intervals.

Involving and working with parents/carers

It is vitally important to work with parents/carers. A similar statement is probably repeated in every book on working with children but it actually makes all the difference. For Pastoral Support Programme meetings (Chapter 7) the effect of gathering everyone together for a supportive and purposeful meeting is most noticeable. Sadly, the effect of not obtaining the participation of parents/carers is equally noticeable. Often schools have tried hard to keep communications going but sheer pressure of work or feelings of helplessness in the face of opposition prevail. There has been an emphasis in recent government initiatives on models that might work to get parents involved. Learning mentors (LM) are one of the strands under the Excellence in Cities (DfEE 1999a) funding. They have a very different role to teachers and more flexible working patterns. Part of their brief is to include parents. They can visit parents and pupils in their own homes, and get involved with the family to encourage attendance at meetings. Some schools have developed a range of successful methods to attract into school parents who are difficult to reach. The approach often involves thinking creatively about what parents might want to get out of the experience, especially if most of their visits to school have been very negative. Some ideas that have worked are:

- running parenting groups in a very supportive and non-judgemental way;
- offering IT and Internet information evenings for parents to learn what their children are doing;
- offering space for parents to run their own regular meeting/social gathering.

Very simple but important ways to encourage parents to remain in contact with the school are:

- Contacting parents with good news as well as bad. A phone call saying what a brilliant day Lucy has had does wonders for home–school relations.
- Ensuring that information sent to parents, especially about meetings they need to attend, is easy to understand and the purposes of the meeting clearly stated. There is nothing more undermining for a parent than to attend what they think is a meeting with the tutor only to discover a whole range of professionals waiting for them.
- Including the parents in discussions when they do attend. They have vital information about their children.

A whole-school approach

Any approach for change in dealing with pupils with emotional and behavioural difficulties should be effectively promoted and supported. There should be a whole-school approach to trying new strategies and adopting flexible approaches to dealing with challenging behaviours.

In research aimed at identifying how mainstream schools achieved effective approaches to the assessment, provision and evaluation of practice for pupils with EBD, five common features were found which all underpin the idea of a whole-school approach.

These can be interpreted as necessary conditions for working effectively with pupils with EBD:

- *Leadership:* Head teachers and senior management teams who provide effective leadership, particularly in communicating the appropriate values, ethos and aspirations of the school.
- *Sharing values:* A core of staff who work together to promote the values of the school, working with all pupils in ensuring these values and aspirations are realised in practice.
- *Behaviour policy and practice:* A consistent and well-monitored behaviour policy where the approaches taken with EBD pupils are an extension of the behaviour policy for all pupils.
- *Understanding EBD:* Key members of staff who understand the nature of emotional and behavioural difficulties, and are able to distinguish these from sporadic misbehaviour or short-term emotional difficulties.

- *Teaching skills and the curriculum:* Effective teaching skills for pupils with EBD are the same as those for all pupils; including the ability to learn from one's own actions, and teaching an appropriately challenging curriculum.

(Daniels *et al.* 1998)

Clearly the words 'challenging behaviour' could be substituted for EBD and the same principles would apply.

The theme of the whole-school approach will be revisited as we look at each stage of the continuum of provision, from early intervention to Pastoral Support Programmes.

For many schools the quantity of new initiatives, though welcome in terms of ideas and funding, have left a feeling of confusion about how to create an effective and streamlined system for meeting the needs of pupils. Some schools have found it useful to draw up a diagram of support and look at all the possible resources available and when they could be utilised. An example of this is shown in Figure 1.3.

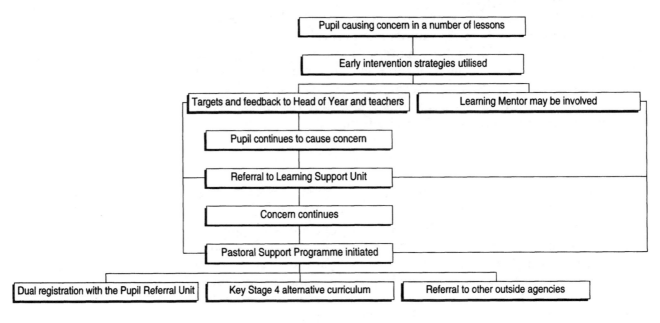

Figure 1.3 School support strategies

Developing such diagrams and linking support strands has proved a very valuable exercise to avoid pupils slipping through the net or conversely accessing everyone at the same time. One strategy is to link all those involved in support into a team, which meets on a regular basis to share information and plan for pupils' individual needs. A common assessment tool and common language for assessing pupils with challenging behaviour at any stage of the continuum is very helpful. The integrated approach can offer concrete evidence on which to base decisions about which support strand to use. If it is used by other institutions it has the added advantage of aiding communication between schools as well as within schools.

The idea of a common language can be taken a stage further and a programme adopted across an LEA that looks at assessment, target setting and strategies for pupils with challenging behaviours across institutions. The advantage of this approach is that it makes movement between institutions smoother, more informed and is likely to be much more successful for pupils. Also, once schools are applying a similar approach, greater sharing of ideas and approaches is possible and communication is greatly enhanced.

One of the aims of the Inclusion Pilot Project in Wandsworth, which was funded through a Standards Fund grant, was to share a common set of criteria for assessing and target setting for pupils with challenging behaviour. Evidence suggests that by providing an inclusion programme for young people who are experiencing problems within a mainstream setting early enough, extreme measures such as exclusion can be avoided in a number of cases. In addition, by using the programme within various settings (mainstream schools, Pupil Referral Units), the development of a common language and set of tools across these settings will be developed which will aid future communication between institutions.

The aims of the project in Wandsworth are:

- To develop an inclusion programme in secondary schools using the same framework for
    assessment
    intervention (group work)
    support (post-intervention)
- To use a common set of criteria across the authority for
    assessment
    target setting
    pupils with challenging behaviour
- Development of communication between institutions using
    common language
    common set of tools
- To help individual schools and the LEA to meet the Social Inclusion: Pupil Support targets.

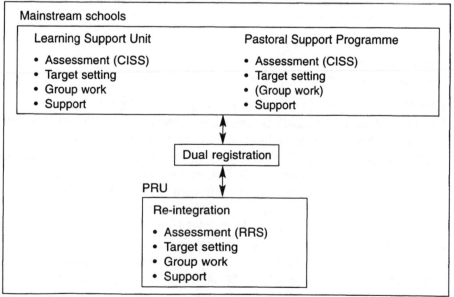

Figure 1.4 Integrated LEA approach: common assessment, common language

In creating an integrated LEA approach the movement of pupils from one institution to another has become more meaningful. The Pupil Referral Unit and the school can start working with a child using information from a programme that all institutions are implementing. It has helped to make the Pastoral Support Programme process a proactive one, with schools increasingly able to access and utilise the range of possibilities for supporting pupils both within schools and jointly with outside provision for pupils who are finding school a challenge. All of these elements will be discussed in more detail in subsequent chapters.

Key points

➤ The approach presented is set in the context of a transactional model.

➤ The approach aims to promote cognitive change.

➤ Involving parents/carers is important to the success of the approach.

➤ Any effective approach needs to be embedded in a whole-school approach.

➤ Linking schools through a whole LEA approach can be very effective.

Food for thought: suggestions for group discussion or further reflection

The language of special needs

As both Corbett (1995) and Armstrong *et al.* (2000) note, there is a specific language of special needs which influences how we perceive the person or the 'problem'. Corbett goes as far as to call this 'Bad Mouthing'. This language of special needs is further reflected for pupils with emotional and behavioural difficulties by a language of blame. Even the labels used tend to lay the 'blame' with the pupils:

- emotional and behavioural difficulties;
- disturbed children;
- in danger of permanent exclusion.

Part of the process of 'inclusion' is shifting our language to incorporate the fact that problems have multiple layers and many facets, of which the pupil is only one part (this links to the idea of a transactional model).

The new guidance 'Social Inclusion: Pupil Support' and 'Social Inclusion: the LEA role in Pupil Support' (DfEE Circulars 10/99 and 11/99) requires schools and LEAs to formulate and implement plans and strategies before a pupil is permanently excluded – plans to prevent this occurring. It is the author's experience that in several schools in various LEAs a shift in attitude has been seen when the implementation of the guidance has been successful. Where the LEA has been proactive in supporting schools in the implementation of the guidance this shift has been greater. This shift in attitude has been reflected, for example, by some schools initially seeing the

Pastoral Support Programmes (PSPs) as just delaying the inevitable. Where the process has been effective there has been a growing realisation of the potential for PSPs to be a powerful process for change in both schools (staff attitudes, staff flexibility, etc.) and pupils (school can work, teachers do care). The success of the process has positive effects on home–school relationships and involvement of outside agencies in a partnership approach.

The effects of such a shift to positive thinking about the process is partly about power relations, moving from an attitude of 'If you don't...you will be...' to 'How can we all work together to improve a difficult situation?' The process of change in schools is all the more remarkable and powerful when considered in the context of increasing selection and competition between schools. It is heartening to work in schools that still take a holistic and community attitude to their pupils and see that throwing your rubbish over the fence is unlikely to equal that problem disappearing!

It is worth remembering that inclusion/exclusion is part of a political process. As Tony Booth (2000) points out, education can be seen as a powerful tool in social cohesion but this is unlikely to be the case unless our schools are inclusive and reflect the social world we all find ourselves living in.

Questions

What sort of language of special needs is used in your school/PRU/LEA? (Try to devise alternative language that is positive rather than negative.)

Are there ways in which your own practice could change to reflect the ideas presented in this chapter?

Is there a negative cycle with one pupil you could start to change?

Are there ways in which the institution in which you work could change to be more inclusive?

What small changes could start the process?

How can you influence colleagues who subscribe to the negative approach?

Chapter 2

The development of the re-integration programme

Questions this chapter aims to answer
How was the original programme devised?
How was the assessment tool developed?
What does the preparation phase consist of?
What are the key aspects of successful support?
Was the programme successful?

Origins of the re-integration process and how it has developed

The programme and the ideas for this book itself have been developed over a number of years of both practical experience and research. Initial concepts have evolved through work in a number of educational settings, including both special and mainstream schools and in joint education and social services settings.

The original re-integration programme was developed at a special school for pupils with emotional and behavioural difficulties (EBD). The school was an all age mixed school, taking pupils from 5 to 16 years of age. It was divided into primary and secondary departments and each aimed to function as closely to a mainstream school as possible. In the primary department classes were taught in the main by their class teacher; in the secondary department the key adult was the tutor and tutor groups were taught by subject specialists and moved around following a timetable for their lessons. The school had an active policy of re-integrating pupils back into mainstream schools where possible. This policy was fairly haphazard in practice.

The programme was developed as part of a research degree with the aim of using the research process to develop and implement a practical tool and set of processes to promote the re-integration of pupils with emotional and behavioural difficulties into mainstream schools. The programme had a three-part structure:

- Assessment
- Preparation (intervention)
- Support

This three-part structure has remained the basis of all the programme's applications.

One of the issues that was raised in staff discussions in the EBD school was how to assess when pupils might be ready for re-integration and how best to prepare them for this transition. The first approach was to design an assessment tool because there was no existing tool for assessing readiness to re-integrate. In the first instance all staff at the special school were asked to list skills that they thought a pupil re-integrating back into a mainstream school would need. The teachers' lists of skills were amalgamated under headings where these had been suggested and given back to all the teachers. There were far too many items in the list so there was a need to reduce the suggestions to those most important, as agreed by all the staff. Staff were therefore asked to rate each item in the list on a scale of 1–10 of importance for successful re-integration, 1 being of no importance and 10 being very important. From this information it was possible to create a number of subsections of items which the teaching staff agreed were the most important. Concurrently with this activity colleagues in mainstream primary and secondary schools were also asked for their lists of skills a pupil would need to re-integrate. The lists from staff in the special school were compared with those from the mainstream to ensure there was agreement. This process was about teachers in various institutions being asked their views and those views being reflected in the completed assessment tool.

The next step was to take a sample of pupils and find out whether the assessment tool actually measured a difference between different groups of pupils: in other words did it have validity? The Re-integration Readiness Scale (RRS), as it was called, was piloted with four groups of pupils as shown in Figure 2.1.

Group design			
A Mainstream successful	B Mainstream borderline	C Possible re-integration	D No re-integration
Number of pupils			
20	20	20	20

Figure 2.1 Group design of original re-integration research

Group design: an explanation

The pupils in groups A and B were from mainstream primary and secondary schools. Teachers were asked to identify children in consultation with their colleagues who fitted into one of the two groups suggested. Group A were pupils who were regarded as successful mainstream pupils. This was not based only on academic success but also on their ability to fit in and make the most of their school experience. Group B were pupils identified by their school as being at risk of school failure because of their emotional and behavioural difficulties. Once the pupils had been identified in consultation with all staff the class teacher or tutor of each pupil was asked to complete the RRS for that pupil.

The pupils in groups C and D were from the special school for children with emotional and behavioural difficulties. All the staff were involved in identifying pupils for each group. Group C were pupils identified as ready to work towards re-integration to a mainstream school. These were pupils who had made specific improvements in their work and behaviour since attending the special school and were being identified by staff as possible candidates for a re-integration programme. Group D were pupils who were considered as not being ready for re-integration at that time. These were pupils who had made no improvement or whose behaviour had deteriorated since arrival at the special school. The pupils were chosen for each group by staff discussion at a meeting where everyone's views and ideas could be shared. The class teacher or tutor then completed the RRS for each identified pupil.

Results

The pilot indicated that the RRS differentiated between these groups of pupils and therefore suggested that it would be appropriate to use it as a tool for measuring 'readiness' to re-integrate. It would be worth adding a word of caution at this stage. The scale was designed to be used as part of a process and not on its own. After readiness to re-integrate was indicated through the use of the RRS, a period of preparation for transfer was undertaken.

The information from the assessment tool can be used in a variety of ways and this is explored in more detail in Chapter 3.

Preparation   Pupil assessment and target setting

Once pupils had been assessed by staff as ready to begin the process of re-integration, they assessed themselves using the RRS. They then set targets based on areas of weakness indicated by their assessment and they joined the 're-integration group'. The pupils then set their own targets using the Pupil Action Plan, which is reproduced as Appendix 1 of this book. Targets were set and then discussed in detail to help pupils develop realistic strategies for achieving their targets. Pupils assessing themselves is an essential part of the programme (more details about this process are given in Chapter 4).

Re-integration group

In this section a brief overview of the key features of the original re-integration group is given. This process is built on and developed in Chapter 4, which looks at the group work process in detail. This group met once a week to set and monitor targets and to work on developing social skills and strategies for coping with situations. The aims of attendance at the group are detailed below.

Re-integration group

The aim of the re-integration group is to:
• raise self-awareness
• foster a positive self-image
• help pupils develop strategies
• enable pupils to set their own targets
• enable pupils to assess their own progress
• prepare for mainstream school.

This group provided an opportunity for pupils with the same long-term aim (mainstream re-integration) to share their fears, hopes and concerns. Pupils could set their own guidelines for group behaviour and format. This approach proved particularly effective as it gave pupils ownership of the process. Time was set aside for discussion of feelings, fears, behavioural strategies and consideration of the future. Once some members of the group were involved in preliminary visits to their proposed school the feedback and discussion generated by this was very beneficial. Some groups of pupils also identified other ideas for group work that they felt would be helpful, including:

• practising reading, writing and spelling;
• drama;
• watching relevant videos.

These activities and discussion sessions were aimed at addressing the first three aims of the group, as shown above.

Pupils in the re-integration group set themselves work and behaviour targets on the Pupil Action Plan (PAP) (Appendix 1). A time-scale was set for the targets. The pupils noted ideas about what they needed to do to achieve their targets and how staff could help them. Each week during the meeting of the re-integration group the pupils discussed their targets and how they had approached and dealt with problems using the PAP. Staff within their daily/weekly meetings discussed the pupils' progress, were made aware of the targets being worked on and offered feedback to the pupils through the coordinating member of staff.

Good working habits and coping skills are very important for successful re-integration. Coping skills which can be usefully looked at in detail in the group are:

• expressing anger appropriately;
• coping with insults;
• coping with being unfairly blamed.

Self-control is an area of particular importance; knowing when you are misbehaving is an important part of self-regulation, as is anticipating the consequences of your own actions. Many pupils found this a difficult area to work on and have to work very hard to acquire successful and usable strategies.

Learning support

Pupils needing additional learning support to boost basic skills before transition should receive extra support in class where possible. It was sometimes appropriate to focus on particular areas of concern through work set in the re-integration group. The work was completed at home or at another time set aside for this purpose. When several pupils were preparing for mainstream re-integration had additional learning problems the group was an ideal place to provide extra help and mutual support.

Length of preparation

Some pupils needed a great deal of preparation. While their scores on the RRS suggested that they had potential for re-integration, they appeared set on some behaviour patterns that were difficult to break. This seems particularly to be the case with irritating/attention-seeking behaviours, e.g. shrieking, tapping, shouting out and humming. These behaviour patterns drew attention to the pupil exhibiting them and needed to be addressed before a mainstream placement could successfully go ahead.

Some pupils identified by the scale and initially positive about mainstream re-integration decide not to re-integrate. Vital components of preparation are addressing fears and worries and accepting the benefits and problems of transfer. Some pupils during the process of preparation decide that they are not ready or that this is not the route they wish to follow. This seems to arise more frequently if the pupil experiences severe learning difficulties (especially literacy problems). Some pupils experience of mainstream schooling has been so negative that the proximity of transfer causes extreme stress and they decide not to continue with the programme.

Parental support

In a small number of cases the parents decide that they do not want re-integration to take place. It is almost impossible to effect a successful transfer without parental support. It is vital to work with parents from the outset and keep them informed so that everyone works in partnership towards the same goal. Including parents in the re-integration process will be discussed in more detail in Chapter 8.

Experience suggests a long period of preparation is preferable, e.g. at least two or three terms.

Support

The third strand to the re-integration programme was support for pupils once they had transferred. Post-re-integration support was vital to the success of the transfer. It offered support for both the pupils and the receiving school. Each pupil received half a day's support each week. A teacher from the special school provided the support. Continuous monitoring was employed to improve the clarity of the support role and successive support was improved over the period. The key aspects are detailed below.

The key aspects of successful support

Prior to transfer
- Support teacher is familiar with the receiving school and has met with key personnel to plan for the pupil's needs prior to the re-integration.
- Pupil is familiar with the support teacher and has visited the new school with the support teacher and parent/carer.
- Pupil has spent time within the class or tutor group he or she will be joining.
- Final planning has taken place after these visits.
- Support is clearly outlined to both receiving school and pupil so that everyone is clear what will happen, and when.
- Records have been passed to receiving school, including RRS data and summary of targets set in re-integration group.

Post-transfer
- Support teacher sets aside time each week to meet with key person in school to discuss pupil's progress and offer advice and support.
- Support teacher keeps a record of pupil's progress and problems encountered.
- Support for pupils will vary depending on individual needs but initially some time spent with the pupil each week to discuss any problems encountered is advisable.

Chapter 8 includes further discussion of support for pupils re-integrating from a Pupil Referral Unit. Post-intervention support at earlier stages of the continuum is also discussed in Chapters 5, 6 and 7.

Success of the programme

The programme was very successful in meeting its original aims; over a four-year period 27 pupils were re-integrated from the EBD special school. Of those re-integrated over this period, 81.5 per cent maintained their mainstream placement. During that four-year period the programme was being developed and refined. Of those who received the fully developed programme, 100 per cent remained in mainstream school at the end of this period.

In 1996 SENJIT published the programme (McSherry 1996). The publication was a summary of the programme developed for use with pupils in the EBD special school who were preparing to return to mainstream school. It was published in response to a well-received presentation of the programme to managers of Pupil Referral Units at a SENJIT (University of London) conference. Pupil Referral Units (PRU) have as part of their brief the task of re-integrating pupils back into mainstream schools and many of the staff in PRUs then and now find this one of the most challenging aspects of their role. The programme was seen as offering a structure to the process and had three stages to facilitate an effective re-integration:

(SENJIT, Institute of Education, University of London, 20 Bedford Way, London, WC1H 0AL. Tel: 020 7612 627314)

- Clear and consistent criteria for assessing readiness.
- A structured programme to prepare pupils for transfer.
- A post-transfer support package that enables both the pupil and the school to experience a positive change over a period.

The application of the full programme to pupils re-integrating from a Pupil Referral Unit is discussed in more detail in Chapter 8.

Key points

➤ The re-integration programme consists of three stages: assessment, preparation and support.

➤ The assessment tool (RRS) was devised in consultation with mainstream and special school colleagues and piloted with four groups of pupils.

➤ Pupils assess themselves using the RRS and set targets from their own ratings.

➤ Pupils monitor and change targets as part of a group.

➤ The group (re-integration group) is part of the preparation process for pupils who are going to re-integrate into a mainstream school.

➤ Parents should be involved at all stages of the process.

➤ Support for pupils re-integrating is vital.

➤ Support should be carefully set up with the receiving school to meet the needs of the pupil.

➤ The support teacher needs to maintain a continuous dialogue with key personnel in the receiving school.

Food for thought

Transfer syndrome

The following case study reflects that of many pupils who start to prepare for mainstream re-integration and then get 'transfer syndrome'. Transfer syndrome reflects the deterioration in behaviour of pupils after they have started to prepare for mainstream transfer. It is almost as if they revert to previous behaviour patterns as a way of avoiding the oncoming crisis (this is the pupil's way of dealing with the anxiety of changing schools). For many pupils their time at the EBD special school or Pupil Referral Unit has been very successful. They have developed socially and emotionally as part of a small group and they have been able to enjoy working relationships with the staff. While they want to access the opportunities offered by a mainstream school they are still understandably terrified of what will happen. The last experience of mainstream school for many of these children had been disastrous and they know they do not want to repeat that experience. It is not advisable to continue with an imminent transfer while the pupil is still in this mode of crisis.

Case Study 2.1

Transfer syndrome

David had been assessed very positively by his teachers on the RRS. He had been at the EBD school for four years and would be re-integrating into a mainstream secondary school in Year 8. David had assessed himself using the RRS and enjoyed reflecting on the improvements he had made. He set himself realistic targets for further improvement and attended the re-integration group regularly.

After five weeks in the group a school placement was found for David and his return to school was planned for a term later. Almost as soon as the placement was found David's behaviour rapidly deteriorated. He began to be sent out of lessons for silly behaviour and was also getting into trouble at lunch-times. He was no longer achieving his weekly targets and was negative in the re-integration group sessions.

Staff in the special school were concerned for David and about his behaviour.

Questions

What would be your action plan for helping David through this phase?

How would you involve all staff in this process?

Could you involve the other pupils in the re-integration group in helping David? (If yes, how might you approach this?)

Chapter 3

Assessment: The Coping in Schools Scale (CISS)

> **Questions this chapter aims to answer**
> What are the aims of the Inclusion Pilot Project in Wandsworth?
> How was the RRS adapted for mainstream use?
> How are data collected using the Coping in Schools Scale?
> How can the information gathered be analysed and used?

The programme in the format described in Chapter 2 has been used in EBD special schools and Pupil Referral Units (PRU) in several LEAs since its publication. Wandsworth LEA was already beginning to use the programme in both the PRU and EBD schools. The aim of the Inclusion Pilot Project (see Chapter 1) was to use the programme as an inclusion tool in mainstream schools and to aid re-integration of pupils from the PRU. This chapter will discuss the assessment tool adapted for mainstream use: the Coping in Schools Scale (CISS). Chapter 4 will look in detail at the group work approach used in schools. The third strand of the programme, support, will be discussed as part of each application of the approach in Part Two (Chapters 5 to 9).

Initial developments from the Re-integration Readiness Scale (RRS)

In the first stages of the project, secondary schools were offered initial training in the use of the original assessment tool (RRS). From this first wave of INSET it was important to encourage practitioner feedback on how the RRS would translate to the mainstream setting. The intention was to establish whether the ideas, as originally developed, could translate to a different setting and still prove useful and effective. Feedback from teachers about the application of the assessment was actively encouraged. The majority of mainstream teachers greeted the idea of a systematic and consistent assessment of pupils' behavioural needs very positively, but an interesting debate soon developed.

As part of the training process teachers were asked to think of a pupil they knew who might be in danger of dropping out/being excluded because of their emotional and behavioural difficulties. Then individually or in groups they completed the RRS. If completed individually they would then compare notes in a group to see if differing views were held. If they completed as a group this discussion and debate would have been part of the original process.

It became apparent that secondary teachers had very different levels of knowledge of particular pupils. A tutor or Head of Year may have no difficulty completing the scale but some subject teachers felt unable to answer questions on aspects of pupil behaviour outside the classroom context. There were also, as could be anticipated, very differing experiences of the same pupil by different teachers. Some teachers also reported difficulty completing the 'Literacy Skills' items. This is an interesting issue as some level of difficulty accessing the curriculum undoubtedly existed for many of the pupils identified. If teachers are not clear about these difficulties it is unlikely that they are able to differentiate the work accordingly. (It might just be worth thinking back to the transactional model presented in Chapter 1 to see how this lack of knowledge and planning might affect interactions between teacher and pupil.) The decision was made to retain 'Learning Skills' as a section, with some items from the 'Literacy Skills' section included, within the shorter version discussed below because it was vital that these issues were reflected upon when planning for pupils' needs.

Practical application of the CISS

An important part of planning any intervention for a pupil, especially a pupil with emotional and behavioural difficulties, is to have as full a picture of the problems as they seem to be manifested and then to build on strengths and/or areas of success. It would seem important therefore to have:

(a) as full a picture of each pupil as possible;
(b) as broad (across subjects) a picture of each pupil as possible.

In order to achieve this and to develop something that was going to work in practical terms in secondary schools two versions of the scale were necessary (full and shorter versions). (See panel.)

Coping in Schools Scale (CISS)

Full version   (8 sections)
Self Management of Behaviour
Self and Others
Self Awareness
Self Confidence
Self Organisation
Attitude
Learning Skills
Literacy Skills

Shorter version   (5 sections)
Self Management of Behaviour
Self and Others
Self Organisation
Attitude
Learning Skills

The longer version is designed for those with pastoral responsibility for the pupil (tutor, Head of Year) who have a depth of knowledge about the pupil. The shorter version is for subject teachers who have a breadth and spread of experience of the pupil. The longer version remained essentially the RRS, with a few items reworded, and became the Coping in Schools Scale (CISS) Full Version (see Appendix 2). The subject teacher's version took those items directly relating to classroom behaviours and became the Coping in Schools Scale (CISS) Shorter Version (Appendix 3). As many teachers as possible who work with the pupil should complete the shorter version so that a profile of the pupil can be put together. This profile includes the teachers' and the pupil's views and helps with planning intervention and support as well as comparing teachers' and pupil's perceptions. (In primary schools the full version of the CISS is used. This is discussed in more detail in Chapter 5.)

The CISS consists of the eight sections (as shown in the panel) that originally existed in the Re-integration Readiness Scale (RRS) in the longer version and the five sections in the shorter version, with items under each heading being scored using the same scoring system as the RRS:

1. Does not fulfil this criterion.
2. Rarely fulfils this criterion.
3. More often than not fulfils this criterion.
4. Almost always fulfils this criterion.

The total possible score on the longer version is 284. The total possible score on the shorter version is 152. The two versions are compared by taking the percentage of the total score achieved by the pupil on each completed version of the scale.

Completion of the CISS

- identifies the profile of a pupil who is causing concern;
- gives staff and pupils clear indications of what needs to be addressed;
- is able to offer an agreed set of criteria and a systematic and consistent way of assessing pupils;
- offers a comparison of perspectives between teachers and pupils.

The two versions have been used extensively in Wandsworth secondary schools and by support services working in secondary schools in several other LEAs. Their use has continued to be developed and expanded. Subsequent chapters will look at some of these developments.

Analysing and using the information from the CISS

There are several ways in which the information from the assessment can be used, as detailed in Figure 3.1.

Types of information and how this can be used	
Information	*Uses of this information*
1. Overall percentage (or raw scores) across subjects or teachers	Planning for intervention and continuation of support involving a range of teachers/subjects and the pupils
2. Individual item agreement across teachers or subjects	Short- and long-term target setting and planning (specific criteria) for pupils and teachers
3. Individual item agreement between teachers and pupils	Levels of shared perception between pupil and teachers important for planning intervention with pupils and teachers
4. Ratings on specific criteria	Pupils set targets from their personal ratings. Profile of strengths and weaknesses for individual pupils helps planning for support and can inform IEP or other planning tools

Figure 3.1 Information gathered and uses of this information

Overall percentage or raw scores across subjects and teachers

Secondary pupils

Information from all who have completed the CISS for an individual pupil can be put on the CISS Score Summary Sheet (Appendix 4). This information can then be viewed and shared at a glance. In the sample data shown in Figure 3.2 you can see a summary of the section totals and final total with the percentage of the possible total that the final total represents. This percentage is a way of directly comparing the full and shorter versions of the scale. There are then a number of things we can do with this information.

We can see at a glance if there are certain subjects where problems seem to occur. There may be a pattern to this or not. It could be that the pupil is finding more structured subjects difficult or it could be the opposite. It could be that there are a few unrelated subjects causing difficulties, in which case it may be personality clashes with certain teachers. Alternatively it may be that all the subjects the pupil does with a particular group (the tutor group for example) are more problematic. In each of these scenarios the information gained helps us to plan in a systematic way for the timing and nature of the support we might offer. It also clearly indicates those subjects where the pupil is doing well. We want to build on this success and also ensure that any support that might involve the pupil missing a lesson is not targeted in lessons that are successful. In the example given in Figure 3.2 we can see there is quite a range of scores, 36 to 78 per cent, suggesting that the pupil is managing reasonably well in some subjects but not in others. There does not seem an obvious pattern although Art, Maths and English are more successful subjects. In fact we want to ensure that this pupil does not miss any English or Art lessons as these are going well. If we wanted to target support, with a learning mentor for example, Spanish would be the best subject to target either in-class or withdrawal support. We can also see at a glance that the pupil's perception of how lessons are going on the whole is not in agreement with the teachers' perceptions.

Name: Tutor Group:

CISS Full Version

Section	Self Management of Behaviour	Self and Others	Self Awareness	Self Confidence	Self Organisation	Attitude	Learning Skills	Literacy Skills	Total	%
Pupil	33	33	14	13	40	34	38	32	237/284	83
Tutor	26	23	8	10	30	24	36	32	189/284	67

CISS Shorter Version

Teacher/ Subject	Self Management of Behaviour	Self and Others			Self Organisation	Attitude	Learning Skills		Total	%
Maths	18	21			22	16	33		110/152	69
Science	16	15			17	16	24		88/110	55
English	19	22			27	21	36		125/152	78
Spanish	10	12			10	10	16		58/152	36
History	10	20			11	15	22		78/152	49
Geography	11	15			19	12	27		84/152	53
PE	16	20			22	15	30		103/152	68
RE	11	14			18	15	32		90/152	59
Art	18	20			22	18	30		108/152	71
Technology	18	16			14	16	20		84/152	52

Range: 36–78%

Figure 3.2 Sample CISS score summary sheet

Primary pupils

For primary pupils the longer version of the CISS is generally used and we would be gathering information from fewer sources. In a primary school those adults with the greatest knowledge of the pupils would complete the CISS and this would include the class teacher and maybe the SENCO and head teacher. If other adults were also involved with the pupil, a classroom assistant for example, then information from them would also be most valuable. More details about gathering and using the information in a primary school is given in Chapter 5 which looks at primary/secondary transfer.

Individual item agreement across teachers and subjects

Using the information from the shorter version CISS we can look in detail at those specific items that teachers agree are areas of weakness. The CISS Shorter Version Summary Sheet (Appendix 5) allows you to look at this summary in conjunction with the pupil's self-rating. If we look at the sample data in Figure 3.3 we can see what level of agreement we have between those teachers rating the pupil.

Of the ten teachers in the sample there is considerable agreement on a number of items. The pupil is obviously exhibiting different behaviour patterns across lessons but there are some behaviours which are proving problematic in a number of lessons.

Teacher Ratings Summary	Pupil Perceptions	
Name:	Tutor Group:	
Number of teachers completing the scale: 10		

Section and item	Number of teacher ratings at 1 or 2	Pupil self rating
Self Management of Behaviour		
Can accept discipline without argument or sulking	6	2
Can arrive and settle down quietly and appropriately	3	3
Does not leave the room without permission	3	4
Can accept changes to plans or disappointment with an even temper	4	4
Does not normally use loud exhibitionist language. Is aware of normal sound levels and can be reminded of them and respond without backchat	4	2
Can ask for help	7	3
Self and Others		
Can behave appropriately in the classroom	6	3
Can accept teacher time needs to be shared	2	3
Can ask a question and *wait* for the answer and *take turns* in question and answer situations	3	4
Has appropriate communication skills: talking, asking questions, listening	4	3
Is able to work in a team	7	4
Can speak to people without resorting to rudeness	3	2
Can work in a group situation	6	3
Self Organisation		
Can work alone without constant attention	6	3
Can listen to explanations and instructions and attempts to act on advice given	4	4
Understands the teacher's role within a mainstream school	5	3
Understands the structure of discipline within a mainstream school – what happens if s/he is late or does not complete work, homework, etc.	6	3
Can constructively use unstructured time in the classroom	7	3
Can organise self and possessions	7	3
Can organise him/herself if help is not available	7	3
Good timekeeping, e.g. prompt arrival at lessons	5	2
Attitude		
Is prepared to work in lessons	6	3
Uses appropriate language and gestures	2	2
Is courteous and shows a positive towards staff	3	2
Can show a positive interest in lessons	7	4
Treats school property with care	2	4
Shows a sense of humour	3	4
Learning Skills		
Reading and numeracy up to a level that can be coped with in mainstream, given some support	1	3
Has developed learning strategies to be able to ask teachers or others for advice when experiencing problems (at own level)	8	3
Does not get up and wander round	5	3
Needs a mainstream curriculum	1	4
Does not get impatient if help is not immediately forthcoming	2	4
Will try to start a task on his/her own	7	4
Is willing to try on his/her own	7	3
Generally cares about the work being done	8	3
Pays attention to class discussions and instructions	5	4
Can read sufficiently well to read basic instructions needed for the completion of the task	0	4
Is willing to spend time working out the instructions	6	4

Figure 3.3 Sample Shorter Version Summary

Individual item agreement between teachers and pupil

If we look at the data in Figure 3.3 we see that we also have the pupil's self-rating for those items in the shorter version. The pupil completes the full version of the CISS and we pull out the information found in the shorter version for this comparison. A rating of 1 or 2 on both versions would indicate that the person completing it felt this behaviour was a problem. On the sample data you can see that there is not much agreement, or level of shared perception, about the problems between the pupil and teachers. However, there are a few areas of shared perception such as 'Can accept discipline without argument and sulking' and 'Good timekeeping, e.g. prompt arrival at lessons', so there is a starting point for target setting.

There can be wide variation in teacher and pupil perceptions of the problem. Some pupils clearly identify the same problems as their teachers; some identify a different set of problems, and some identify no problems at all. Any of these patterns give us important information and indicate a starting point for working with individual pupils.

Ratings on specific criteria

Using the pupil's self-ratings, targets are set with the help of a supportive adult. These targets can also be used to inform an Individual Education Plan or other planning tools. It is also important to recognise areas of strength as well as areas of weakness. Areas of strength can be built on and used to help pupils develop strategies for tackling more difficult areas.

> **Key points**
> ➤ The Inclusion Pilot Project in Wandsworth aimed to share a common set of criteria for assessment and target setting for pupils with challenging behaviour to aid inclusion and re-integration.
> ➤ The RRS was adapted for mainstream use to reflect teachers' different levels of knowledge about individual pupils.
> ➤ There are two versions of the assessment tool for mainstream use. The Coping in Schools Scale (CISS) full version is for use by the pupil and either class teacher (primary) or tutor (secondary). The shorter version is for use by subject teachers and is used mainly in secondary schools.
> ➤ The information gathered can be used in a number of ways: to plan for intervention strategies; for target setting and to inform other planning tools (IEPs); to gauge levels of shared perceptions between teachers and between teachers and the pupil.
> ➤ The Coping in Schools Scale itself and summary sheets for gathered information are included in the Appendices.

Food for thought

Questions

Given the sample data used in this chapter in Figures 3.2 and 3.3 (or some of your own gathered using the CISS), how might you start to plan an intervention for this pupil?

If you were working with a pupil who had a very different perception of what the problem was, how would you start to work with him or her?

How might the information you have from the pupil's rating of him or herself inform how you plan with colleagues for supporting this pupil?

Chapter 4

The group work approach

Questions this chapter aims to answer
Why use group work with pupils with challenging behaviour/emotional and behavioural difficulties?
What are the aims of this supportive approach?
How could group work be put into practice, i.e. what are the stages of the group work approach advocated?
What support would staff need in adopting this approach?

Chapter 3 looked at the assessment stage of the process. This first stage is applied at the beginning of any intervention. The second part of the programme is the group work. This is part of a planned intervention that should also include looking in detail at which areas of the curriculum are working well for individual pupils and areas where additional support or a change of groups may be beneficial. Working in groups and developing peer support are important elements of the programme. This chapter looks in detail at the approach used to introduce pupils to a group, and how to set up and maintain a group.

Definition of the group work approach

The group work approach advocated here uses a small group as the basis of work on social skills and coping techniques. The approach aims to develop social skills through interaction with peers and adults in a supportive environment. The aim is to help pupils to reflect on their skills in tackling difficult situations and promote the use of peer support to develop effective strategies. The group work approach described and discussed in this chapter can, and does, take place in a variety of settings, including mainstream secondary schools, mainstream primary schools, Learning Support Units within mainstream schools, Pupil Referral Units and special schools. It is facilitated by a supportive adult and is generally attended by four to six young people. If possible it takes place at the same time and in the same place once a week. Once the group is established it is important to be as consistent as possible in the composition of the group. Any changes to the group's structure should be agreed with all group members so that an individual's confidence, once established, is not undermined.

One of the most rewarding ways of being a successful student is to have the support of your peers, or at least a small but positive group of them. Harry Potter, on losing the support of his friend Ron in *Harry Potter and the Goblet of Fire* (Rowling 2000), goes through one of his most miserable times at school so far. Many pupils with challenging behaviour do not have the positive support of their peers. They may use bad behaviour to secure the support and credibility of a group of peers, those who are also disenfranchised and on the periphery of the school system. The power of having others wanting them to do well is a turning point for many pupils. For others to care enough to look out for them is reward in itself.

One way of attempting to set up a peer support system is through the use of small, well-managed group work. Pupils can learn how to help and support each other with (and through the example of) a supportive adult. This adult could be a teacher or a learning mentor, someone to whom the pupils can look for guidance and support. Some pupils will struggle against allowing someone to offer this support. Their experience of adult support may be inconsistent and frightening and they may have become very adept at building barriers. By not allowing anyone to break through their barriers they may be preventing further disappointment. It can be very frustrating working with emotionally damaged pupils. Keeping hold of the idea that this may be a very frightening experience for the young person helps to place and maintain the apparent rejection of your efforts in context.

There are some very important 'rules' about this type of group work approach. If we hope to offer consistency we have to commit ourselves to a specific time and place for the group to meet. In a busy secondary school where time and space are at a premium this can sometimes be difficult. If staff and pupils alike experience that this prerequisite is constantly tampered with, the group will have little chance of succeeding, which will lead to frustration. Schools need to commit resources (staff, time and space) if the group work is to be a successful strategy.

It is also important that the group membership is static. If new students are to join the group then this should be discussed and agreed by all. As an example of this, if someone (often a visiting teacher or educational psychologist) asks to visit the group this should always be agreed with all the group members in a group session. It should also be clearly explained what the visitor does and how they may want to use their experience of visiting the group, i.e. to set up their own group.

It is important that confidentiality is agreed within the group so that group members can feel confident to discuss issues that arise.

Rationale for the group work approach

> Since most human problems arise in the setting of group life, many can be solved in a group setting. (Dwivedi 1993)

One of the important features of the Coping in Schools programme is the use of group work as a method of support and intervention. The use of group work is very powerful. It encourages reflection, builds

The Coping in Schools programme and group work

peer support and develops peer relationships. For most of the students who may require help at any stage of the continuum illustrated in Figure 1 (page 2), a need to develop their group working skills will be apparent. It is not always the case that students can work in groups. They may need to be introduced gradually to working with others through the use of pairs before joining a larger group.

Group work has been used widely in therapeutic settings and its benefits have been discussed in this context (Dwivedi 1993). School-aged children spend most of their lives in group settings of some sort and it is important for their success in the school setting that they can function effectively as part of a group. The use of small group work in secondary schools is less widely used but is beginning to achieve more prominence (Decker *et al.* 1999).

This programme, with its emphasis on the value of group work, has been used as part of an action research pilot project across all the secondary schools in one LEA, for pupils at various stages of the continuum (Figure 1). Initial evaluations would indicate that pupils who participate find it helpful, parents are very positive about the input their child has received and mainstream teachers find it useful for target setting and in developing an improved understanding of EBD.

The function of the group work is to:

- raise self-esteem;
- foster a positive self-image;
- help pupils to develop strategies;
- enable pupils to set their own targets;
- enable pupils to assess their own progress;
- develop the support and help of others in the group;
- offer positive reinforcement for pupils' successes.

It is important that small group work is tailored to pupils' concentration levels and their communication abilities. Use of activities to promote social skills such as games, role-play and art work can be beneficial.

Many teachers are concerned about the running of small groups. Small group work requires a different approach from class teaching:

(a) the functioning of the group is the focus, rather than the curriculum content of the session;
(b) it requires a flexibility of approach, e.g. non-directive interaction;
(c) it requires a different relationship with the young people in the group;
(d) it is more difficult to plan and predict;
(e) it needs consistency in time, place and personnel;
(f) it will be a difficult experience initially for many of the young people;
(g) it is important to understand that change may appear to be slow.

If you wish to add a framework to initial sessions you can either use published resources or develop your own. The emphasis of these should be fun, as well as asking some of the important questions that you need to address with the group. A list of useful published resources is included at the end of this chapter.

Whether you use your own or published resources to add a framework initially to a new group, the aims of the group work remain the same and should influence the way you plan to run your groups.

Stages of the group work process

1. Pupil completes the CISS with a member of staff.
2. Pupil sets a target based on their rating of themselves.
3. Pupil joins a group (or pair) on a weekly basis.
4. Pupil assesses towards his or her own progress targets and discusses this with other group members.
5. Pupils offer help and support to other group members.

---

1. Pupil completes the CISS with a supportive adult

Initiating the relationship

Completing the CISS with a pupil can be the first extended contact that the supportive adult has with a particular pupil. This approach works very well and is a constructive way of initiating the relationship. In a number of schools learning mentors have used the CISS as the basis of a structured interview with a pupil at the beginning of their input.

It can also work well if the pupil is familiar with the supportive adult. However, if this is a change of role for the teacher in relation to the pupil some preliminary explanation and discussion about this new role will be required. Both teacher and pupil are beginning a new relationship and this needs careful handling.

Introducing the task

Some explanation of the CISS is needed as a way of introducing the task and it is best to keep this as simple as possible. One approach is to introduce the CISS as a way of finding out what the pupil thinks they are good at and what they might find difficult in school. Some pupils will never have been asked their opinion of the problems before and are keen to express their opinion. Others may be reluctant to admit any areas of difficulty and rate themselves very positively on all items. At this early stage it is important to allow the pupils to *rate themselves as they see it*, or to the level that they are prepared to admit to at this stage. Even if you feel the view the pupil is presenting is not accurate, at this stage this is not particularly relevant – *it is their view that is being sought*. Valuing their perceptions is the first step towards raising self-esteem.

Completing the CISS

The scale is designed to be completed by the pupil with an adult to assist and guide. A deliberate decision has been made not to develop a separate assessment tool in child-friendly language because pupils assessing themselves on their own is not the object of the exercise. To

Stages of the group work process

see the process as a structured interview or a guided conversation to enable the pupil to complete the scale would perhaps be the easiest way of describing the process. It is advisable to familiarise yourself with the CISS before embarking on the process with a pupil. You may want to jot down some concrete examples of situations where the behaviours in question could occur, to use if pupils ask for clarification.

Skills of self-assessment

Some pupils are very clear about their strengths and weaknesses and complete the CISS with confidence and self-awareness. Other pupils are either unaware of the effects of their behaviour or are only able to rate themselves positively at this early stage. It is their perceptions of themselves at a point in time. What is important is that confidentiality and support are stressed and that pupils feel encouraged to be reflective about their behaviour and its effects through the group work process. It can be the case that a pupil asks to change their original rating after being in a group for a few weeks. Perhaps at this stage they feel confident enough to start to see how they themselves are part of the process.

2. Pupils set targets based on their ratings of themselves

Behaviour target

Pupils choose an area on which to work, using their ratings of themselves on the CISS with the help of the supportive adult who has assisted them in completing the scale. They set a specific target on which to work for a number of weeks. Many pupils need help in developing specific and manageable targets. The pro-forma that has been developed is shown as Appendix 1. The first target discussed is a behaviour target. As an example let us assume that one of the areas of concern raised by the pupil was arriving for lessons on time. If the pupil were at present not arriving for any lessons on time it would be unrealistic to set as a target 'Arrive at lessons on time.' It would be more realistic to discuss with the pupil how many lessons we might aim for to achieve success in this week.

It might be useful to explore a few questions with the pupil to focus on reasons for lateness. Is there a pattern to the lateness? Is it worse after break or lunch? Are they late for school in the morning or does the problem only start after arrival at school? What do they think might be the reasons for late arrival at lessons?

Using another example, a primary pupil might say that they find it difficult not to run out of the classroom when they get upset. We may need to establish how frequently they think this is happening. If it occurs daily we may want initially to set one day in the next week in which the pupil will aim to remain in the class for the whole day. If it is happening infrequently, we may want the pupil to try and think what happens before it occurs and set a different target level. If it is usually triggered by comments of peers we may want to talk about strategies for dealing with the anger/upset generated without walking out.

Pupils often have quite clear and interesting reasons for their behaviour. Some of the reasons might be quite surprising. Some might prompt the need for school action as well as or instead of pupil action.

Work target

You would need to use your judgement at this initial stage as to whether to encourage the pupil to set a work target as well. This will depend on how you think each individual pupil is coping with the target setting process itself as well as how you think they will cope with a number of targets. You will need to discuss this with the pupil and come to a decision together. You can leave the work target for the second round of target setting, which will take place after a few weeks. The work target, like the behaviour target, needs to be small, measurable and achievable.

What do I need to do to achieve my targets?

An important part of the target setting process is to reflect on what is stopping the pupil achieving this target at the moment. To use the example of arriving for lessons on time, a number of reasons why the pupil is late could emerge from your discussions. It will be important, in light of the reasons, to decide whether, for example, the issue is getting up in the morning or smoking a cigarette in the toilet on the way to lessons. Reflecting on possible reasons will help the pupil devise specific strategies to avoid the problems identified.

Using the primary school example of running out of the classroom, we might find from discussion that the pupil is finding the whole experience of school too much to cope with all day. We may want to suggest that they ask for permission to take time out and keep their teacher informed of where they are going. The teacher will be able to encourage less frequent or shorter periods of time out of the classroom.

How can staff help me?

Interestingly this section is often the most difficult for pupils to complete. It is designed to encourage pupils to reflect on how staff could help and what help they would welcome. For example, we may think that verbal positive encouragement of pupils for achieving their target would be encouraging but the pupil may not find this helpful at all. As we congratulate them on their early arrival for our lesson today they may see this as emphasising the fact they were late yesterday. If we are aware of the pupil's alternative interpretation we can offer the intended praise in a different way. This 'reframing' (Molnar and Lindquist 1989) of actions as another sees them is salutary for both staff and pupils. The reframing technique is base on four basic propositions:

> (i) we behave in accordance with the way in which we interpret a problem situation, (ii) there are often many different but equally valid interpretations of any given situation, (iii) change our interpretation and we can change our behaviour and (iv) change in our behaviour will influence the perceptions and behaviour of others.
> (Cooper *et al.* 1994)

The above is an example of a practical application of the transactional model discussed in Chapter 1.

3. Pupil joins group (or pair) on a weekly basis

Pairs

Once the pupil has completed the CISS and set a target with the supportive adult, the aim would be to join a group for weekly target monitoring and development of strategies. Some pupils are not ready to join a group immediately and so a first step on this path might be to join with one other pupil in a supported pair. The aim would be to prepare this pair to join a group within a few weeks if possible. It is very informative for the adult to see how the pupil behaves in the company of another. It also allows pupil–adult relationships to focus on positive interaction before joining the larger group.

Why work in a group?

As stated at the beginning of this chapter, it is important for pupils to be able to form constructive and supportive relationships with their peers. However, some pupils find this very difficult for a variety of reasons. Working in a supported small group enables them to be with others and work with others on a clearly defined but informal basis. The process aims to enable pupils to reflect on how others see them as well as on how to relate more constructively towards others. Group work provides the opportunity to practise social skills, to collaborate with others, to negotiate, to discuss strategies, to share concerns, to find ways to develop self-control and to experience positive relationships with adults. You can probably add to this list and certainly as you develop your own group work you will find other areas which you feel can be developed in this context.

4. Pupil assesses progress towards targets and discusses it with group members

Monitoring targets

Pupils use the weekly group meeting to discuss and monitor their targets. It is important to emphasis that the pupil is monitoring and assessing themselves in the company of a small group of peers and a non-judgemental adult. This may require a conscious change in the strategy of the adult (and this is hard to do if you know the pupil has had a bad week). Some pupils may find it difficult at first to discuss their target or their progress with others in the group, and for a few pupils you may have to provide some individual time, but hopefully, if you have progressed pupils through the paired work before embarking on the group, this problem will not arise. At the group meeting each pupil gets the opportunity to feed back to their peers and the supportive adult how they think they have progressed with their target during the last week. If you are positive and identify any achievements while being neutral about difficulties, pupils are generally very honest about their progress. It may be worth obtaining feedback, on a regular basis, from relevant staff so that you are aware if the pupil is either misrepresenting the week's events or is unaware of the effects of certain behaviours. You may have to think carefully about how you are going to use this information to help the pupil set achievable targets. If you have received positive feedback or comments from people outside the group during the week it is useful to feed this back at an appropriate moment. When doing this try to be aware of whether individual pupils prefer a quiet word of feedback or group acknowledgement for this additional feedback. One of the aims of developing this feedback between peers is to develop peer support for group members.

5. Pupils offer help and support to other group members

Promoting peer support

As the group develops an identity and pupils increasingly feel ownership of the process they will begin to offer each other support and strategies for meeting targets. One of the most rewarding aspects of facilitating these groups is enabling pupils to be supportive of each other and to receive support in an appropriate way. It is generally the case that pupils have different starting points and so are very capable of developing strategies appropriate to others. Feedback received from staff trained in using this programme is how surprised they are that the pupils can be so positive and supportive of each other. It is important that we develop these skills and appreciate them.

Planning effective and integrated intervention for pupils

Some pupils receiving the group work approach may also be using other support such as a Learning Support Unit or learning mentor. It is important that all strands of the support offered to students are considered together and complement each other. In some schools this consideration of the various strands of support now available has led to replanning structures within the school's support and discipline process and in others to rewriting the behaviour policies to take these new developments into account.

Support for teachers setting up group work

Having looked in detail at the process for setting up a group and supporting pupils it is worth reflecting on what the adults running the group might need in terms of support.

If it is possible to start running your group with another member of staff this is very helpful. It enables you to discuss and develop ideas together and offer each other support for developing a new approach. It also provides pupils with an experience of two adults relating to each other and modelling ways of discussing/negotiating. This is an active strategy to provide pupils with challenging behaviour with positive role models and ideas for developing constructive relationships. (You may be able to enlist the support of someone from your LEA support services, who has experience of running groups, to work with you on setting up the group). If you are running the group on your own then you need to have someone with whom you can discuss the group on a regular basis (preferably weekly). This person needs to understand and believe in the effectiveness of this approach.

Planning and evaluation

You will need to plan your aims for each session. Although the overall aims will remain the same there may be specific issues that come up one week that need to be addressed the next, or strategies you wish to try to enhance the way the group is functioning. Examples of questions you will probably need to ask yourself are:

What is the aim of this session?
Are there any materials that are needed or might be useful?
Is feedback from other staff required?

You will need to keep a record of group outcomes, including:

Who attended each session.
How each pupil responded to the rest of the group, target monitoring and any planned activities.
Your own responses.
Actions needed as a result of group work.

Over time you will need to evaluate how the group sessions are working for individual pupils. You may need to consider:

Who is attending and responding to the group work.
Who isn't, and the possible reasons for this (you may have been quite explicitly told by the pupil).
Whether the timing of the sessions is working.
Progress on the stated aims.
Your qualitative evaluation of how the group is progressing.

Key points

➤ Group work is an important feature of the Coping in Schools programme.
➤ Developing positive peer support for pupils who are finding school difficult is a valuable strategy.
➤ The group work is positive and supportive and aims to raise pupils' self-esteem and help them develop coping strategies.
➤ There are a number of stages to follow in setting up effective group work:
　(i) Pupils are fully involved in rating themselves using the CISS and setting targets.
　(ii) Pupils may work in pairs before joining a group.
　(iii) Pupils monitor their own progress
➤ Teachers setting up a group work approach will need support.

Food for thought

Case Study 4.1

School A

School A, after the appointment of a new learning mentor and the start of its Learning Support Unit, was finding a level of confusion in both staff and pupils as to what each support strand might offer and how they could be combined. The school had received input from the Coping in Schools project team the term before and wanted to also include the CISS and programme as part of this continuum. It was suggested that as a first stage all the interested and involved parties should meet around a table and look at what they were offering and how this might be developed to offer a cohesive and planned continuum for the student in the school.

As the round table meetings progressed it became apparent that the school's behaviour policy also needed updating to take into account the additional resources and strategies now available. As a parallel to this series of discussions within a small group it was also considered desirable to seek the views of the staff as a whole and to include this in future developments.

A behaviour audit was conducted through which the views of all the staff were requested by questionnaire, to be completed anonymously. Also, half the staff were interviewed to obtain their views in more detail. Again, this was anonymously presented in the summary format.

It was also important to link the new behaviour policy and intervention strands to the Code of Practice to assist staff in adequately meeting a child's special educational needs.

It was therefore decided to plan for supporting a pupil from the early intervention stage with the CISS and programme and to progress to the LSU if this proved inadequate support, and from there to move to a PSP if additional outside help was needed. The learning mentor could be part of a small group work approach at both the early intervention stage and as a post-LSU support strand. It was decided that Heads of Year would offer group work as part of the pastoral programme and that the project team would support this. In this way the group work approach could be offered to quite a number of students as an early intervention and follow-up strategy.

The behaviour audit continued parallel with this process and the results of this were fed back to the staff group as a whole.

Questions

Is there a group of teachers or learning mentors in your school/unit who might be interested in starting some small group work?

How might you offer each other support in introducing this approach?

How might the systems in your school/unit for meeting the needs of these pupils be enhanced by this approach?

How would you feed back targets and progress to your staff group as a whole to ensure that everyone is fully informed of your work?

Books and games useful for developing group work

This list includes a range of resources and styles for use with pupils. Hopefully you will find something inspiring and appealing. There are also a number of publishers or directories that offer wider selections of material to choose from.

Zero tolerance to bullying, Chris Ball and Mary Hartley, 1999. The Chalkface Project, PO Box 1, Milton Keynes, MK5 6JB, 01908 340340. Other books are available in this series

'Retracking', a photocopiable resource pack aimed at promoting student effectiveness, 1996. South Devon Psychological Service, Kennicott Lodge, Ashburton Road, Totnes, TQ9 5JY, 01803 863481.

Developing healthy self-esteem in adolescents, Mary Karsten, 1995. Good Apple.

Everybody wins! 100 games children should play, Dianne Schilling and Terri Akin, 1993. Interchoice Publishing.

Feeling good about yourself, Debbie Pincus, 1990. Good Apple.

Improving communication skills, John Gust, J. Meghan McChesney and Risa R. Gechtman, 1997. Teaching and Learning Company.

Thinking, feeling, behaving: An emotional education curriculum for adolescents, Anne Vernon, 1989. Research Press.

Available from Incentive Plus, 2e Fernfield Farm, Whaddon Road, Little Horwood, Milton Keynes, MK17 0PS, 01908 526120. Incentive Plus markets a range of resources, some of which are listed above.

The Self Esteem Directory, compiled by the Self-Esteem Network, 1997. Smallwood Publishing.

'The Ungame', a board game designed to facilitate communication.

'Esteem Builders Complete Programme', Michele Borba, including books, tapes and activities. Jalmar Press.

Available from Smallwood Publishing, The Old Bakery, Charlton House, Dour Street, Dover, Kent, CT16 1ED, 01304 226800. Smallwood Publishing specialises in books and materials addressing mental health issues. Some examples are listed above.

Managing children, managing themselves: Strategies for the classroom and playground, Teresa Bliss, 1994. Lucky Duck.

Crucial Skills: an anger management and problem solving teaching programme for secondary pupils, Penny Johnson and Tina Rae.

Available from Lucky Duck Publishing, 34 Wellington Park, Clifton, Bristol, BS8 2UW, 01454 776620 or 0117 973 2881. Lucky Duck also publish a range of Circle Time resources.

Part Two

Applications of the programme

Chapter 5

Primary secondary transfer

Questions this chapter aims to answer
What can we do to assist pupils with emotional and behavioural difficulties with their transfer to secondary school?
What preparation can we offer before they transfer?
What support will they need after transfer?

Early intervention	Learning Support Unit	Pastoral Support Programme	Pupil Referral Unit
Coping in School Scale (CISS) and programme	Referral process Coping in School Scale (CISS)	Systematic assessment Coping in School Scale (CISS)	Re-integration programme Re-integration Readiness Scale (RRS)
	Intervention programme	Target setting	Group work
Code of Practice (COP) Stage 2 (New COP School Action)	Code of Practice (COP) Stage 3 (New COP School Action Plus)	Code of Practice (COP) Stage 3 (New COP School Action Plus)	

Re-integration	Re-integration	Re-integration
SUPPORT		

Figure 5.1 A continuum of support for pupils with emotional and behavioural difficulties

As we continue to work with pupils who are having difficulties at the secondary phase it becomes increasingly apparent that one strand of work which needs development is work on the transfer from primary to secondary school. Most pupils find this transfer stressful even if they are also excited and generally very positive about the move. For pupils who have already experienced problems at primary school this is less likely to be the case. Even if they anticipate a new start it is fraught with possible difficulties. Pupils with emotional and behavioural difficulties find this transfer particularly worrying. They often experience difficulties with making friends and with forming trusting adult relationships and these are two activities they will have to do in abundance on arrival at secondary school. These are the sort of worries pupils supported at this transfer stage have voiced:

'There will be so many teachers and they will expect something different.'

'How will I remember which subject each teacher teaches?'

'Other kids will know I have been naughty before and see if they can make me lose it.'

'Where will I go if things go wrong?'

'Older kids put your head down the toilet.'

'Some teachers are mean. What will I do if they pick on me?'

The differences between primary and secondary schools in organisation could not be more different. Although we are all aware of these differences, it sometimes helps when working with pupils to remind ourselves of the complete nature of the transition we ask pupils to make (see panel).

Behaviour support teams, SENCOs, learning mentors and other support staff in secondary schools are increasingly being asked to assist secondary staff with planning for pupils who have found it difficult making this transfer. Often it is the case that pupils have had

Primary school	Secondary school
Head teacher is usually seen by the pupils each day.	Many pupils report not seeing the head teacher from one week to the next.
Head teacher often know all the pupils by name and can talk to them about their families and interests.	Head teacher of a large secondary school will know a few pupils well and others hardly at all.
Schools are generally smaller than secondary schools. Often Key Stage 1 and 2 are on different sites or in different schools.	Schools are often large, many in excess of 1,000 pupils.
Pupils have one teacher for the year who teaches them the majority of subjects.	Pupils may be taught by ten or more teachers in a week, not including their tutor and Head of Year.
Pupils are taught with the same class of pupils for most lessons.	Pupils may be with different groups of peers for most lessons.
Pupils stay in the same classroom for most lessons.	Pupils are expected to navigate their way around a large building at each lesson changeover.
Equipment needed for most lessons is provided and kept in the room.	Pupils are expected to bring their own equipment and to remember which day they need to bring it. They are also expected to carry it around with them all day.
Pupils in Year 6 are the oldest and most knowledgeable pupils in the school.	Pupils in Year 7 are the youngest and least knowledgeable in the school.

problems at primary schools and the primary school would, if asked, have been able to predict some areas of need. There are often issues with the length of time it takes for records to follow pupils and planning on this basis for a child who would need some support immediately at secondary school is obviously not possible. Some secondary schools have very good relationships with their main primary feeder schools and much time and preparation goes into the sharing of information at transfer. Some secondary schools have a very great number of feeder schools and this is of course more problematic. In each authority the picture will vary greatly from school to school.

The structured process suggested in this chapter has been used as part of a primary/secondary transfer project that was used in one LEA. Its main aim was to pilot an approach that potentially could be used across the LEA for identifying pupils with emotional and behavioural difficulties who might need additional support at the secondary transfer stage of their school career. By highlighting pupils' needs in this way secondary schools and support services are enabled to target resources more effectively for pupils in the first few terms of secondary transfer.

As the Coping in Schools programme was being used with success in secondary schools this model was also used as the basis for the transfer process.

The aims of the transfer process are:

Pupil transfer process

- To raise the profile of pupils who may have difficulty with the transfer because of their emotional and behavioural difficulties.
- Data gathering to inform preparation.
- Working with parents/carers to facilitate the transfer of their children.
- To plan for the needs of these pupils both pre-transfer and post-transfer.
- Linking with key staff in each of the secondary schools.
- Pre-transfer intervention.
- Post-transfer support.

Stages of the transfer process

At primary school
School identifies pupils at risk
Parental involvement
Teachers assess pupil using CISS
Pupils complete CISS with a supportive adult
Pupils set targets based on CISS data
Pupils join a preparation group
Secondary school visits
Information sharing with parents

At secondary school
Group work continues
Targets set and monitored
Referral to other in-school support if appropriate

There are various ways this transfer process can be implemented. What steps you take within each stage may depend on whether you are a teacher within the school, either primary or secondary, carrying out the work, or whether you are a member of a behaviour support team, educational psychologist or other support worker from outside the school helping the school to initiate this process. Where relevant, specific issues that may arise for either category will be raised. In the primary/secondary transfer project which the author coordinated an inclusion team worked with schools to implement the process. However, the idea was always to assist in developing a process that schools themselves could implement after training.

Stages of the transfer process – at primary school

School identifies pupils at risk

Primary schools identify those pupils they think are at risk of failing at the transfer stage because of their emotional and behavioural difficulties. If you are a teacher in a primary school initiating this process you will need to discuss with your colleagues who teach Year 6 which pupils are considered at risk. You could do this individually or as part of a staff meeting where all staff can be involved in the initiative. If you are a professional from outside the school setting up this process with primary and secondary schools, then you will need to consider the following steps.

Approach to primary schools
1. Letter to schools with an explanation of the proposed process for gathering information and offering support for group work.
2. After schools have had time to receive and read the letter it is useful to contact schools to arrange to go in person and discuss the process.
3. Meeting in schools with head teacher, SENCO, and Year 6 teachers if possible, to discuss the proposed programme and clarify the objectives of the process.
   Who will be involved?
   When will it take place?
   Where will it take place?
4. You will probably need to set a deadline for lists of identified pupils and completed CISS so that everyone is aware of their roles.

Parental involvement

It is very important that parents/carers are part of any initiative of this sort. In the primary/secondary transfer project in Wandsworth outside support was offered to the school. There is a need to get parental permission for their child's involvement. Most behaviour support services have clear procedures for working with pupils in schools. Parents were initially sent a letter indicating that the school had been fortunate to be part of a project assisting pupils with preparation for their transfer to secondary school. It was then stated that their child would be offered some additional support as part of this project if they were happy with this idea. Parents were asked to complete a permission slip to indicate that their child could participate in this project. Parents were also offered an opportunity to meet the project team and ask any questions. The majority of parents completed the forms and asked for no further information. Some asked further questions and expressed their satisfaction that extra preparation of this sort was on offer. A few failed to return the forms. Some schools followed this up and others did not. Very few parents said they did not want their child to participate.

When starting an initiative of this kind yourself, it is important to think through the possible responses of parents/carers. Sometimes input we perceive as positively beneficial may appear threatening and unnecessary and it is important to address any concerns raised. One way might be to invite parents in for an information morning or evening when the aims of the process are clearly explained and questions can be answered. If the parents have already developed a trusting relationship with an adult in the school, that person should also be involved in the process.

Teachers assess pupil using CISS

It is clear that one important element in planning for a pupil's transfer is relevant information. The CISS used in Year 6 gives a baseline profile of strengths and weaknesses at this stage of primary school. This information can be used for a number of purposes. It clearly shows the areas of concern that the teacher and those involved with the pupil have. This information is useful to secondary teachers in evaluating where support might be needed and what sort of support might be appropriate.

Who should complete the Scale?
Certainly the Year 6 teacher should complete the full version of the CISS. The views of the people giving special needs support are also important. Again the full version should be used. In some schools it might be felt that the head teacher or SENCO have extensive knowledge of the pupil and their views would also be relevant. You may decide to use the shorter version with these additional adults if you are going to ask a range of people (ideally the full version is completed by all, but pragmatically you need to decide how to get the maximum information with the minimum upheaval). The fuller the profile we create using the CISS the better. It is often the case that views held by the adults involved may differ and this is helpful in assessing whether the pupil behaves differently in different contexts.

If you are part of a support service offering to support a number of schools with the transfer process you will need to prioritise your resources somehow. You will probably need to ask teachers to complete the CISS on those pupils whom they are concerned about and then decide which pupils you can best support with a group work approach or on an individual basis. This selection will need to be made in consultation with the school.

1. Analyse CISS data and make decision on appropriate referrals from each school.
2. Visit schools with list, share decisions made and allocation of pupils to groups.

You may decide not to contact parents until you have selected the pupils who you plan to support.

Pupils complete CISS with a supportive adult

Primary pupils may need more help than older pupils with completing the CISS. The way to view it is as a structured interview of guided questions. It is advisable to familiarise yourself with it before using it with pupils. You may want to jot down some concrete examples of situations where the behaviours in question could occur, to use if pupils are asking for clarification.

The pupil's own rating as noted in other applications of the CISS is important for a number of reasons:

• It keeps the pupil central to the process.
• It helps pupils to own the process.
• It promotes discussion between the pupil and an adult about the pupil's strengths and weaknesses.
• It enables the pupil to voice concerns or fears.
• It indicates where the pupil perceives a problem to be.
• It helps to evaluate whether the teacher and pupil have shared perceptions of need.

The majority of primary pupils who have participated in this process greatly enjoy completing the CISS with an adult. They often have clear ideas about themselves and their behaviour and frequently offer perceptive insights into the problems that they experience. With primary pupils, as with secondary pupils, the full version of the CISS should be used.

Analysing the data you have collected

By this stage you have information from the teacher, other involved adults in the school and the pupil. You can now look at this to see the level of shared perceptions between the adults and between the adults and the pupil. (For examples of data see Chapter 3, Figures 3.2 and 3.3.) Levels of shared perception are important. If there is no agreement between the adults and the pupil, the pupil is either unaware of the effect their behaviour is having on others or unable at this stage to express that awareness. Either way they may feel very angry about the response they are receiving and this will need to be explored. Having the view of several adults is always helpful in ascertaining if part of the problem is the relationship between the child and a particular adult, for whatever reason, or a more general problem.

Pupils set targets based on CISS data

After rating themselves pupils are then helped to set an appropriate target to work on. As indicated in previous chapters, pupils often need guidance to set a realistic and manageable target. The aim is to set a target which is achievable in the short term. You may have to break down target behaviours into smaller steps. So for example, if a pupil frequently leaves the room without permission a first step might be to reduce the frequency of this behaviour. Alternatively it might be that when they leave the room there is a designated place for them to go to, a chair outside or a central area where they can be seen. In effect they have got the teacher's permission because they agree to go to a particular place. This strategy can be a useful first step that enables a pupil to leave a difficult situation but also for the teacher to have control over where that pupil is going. Further guidance on target setting using the CISS is given in Chapter 4.

Pupils join a preparation group

The preparation group follows the same format as those discussed in previous chapters (Chapter 4 contains detailed guidelines on setting up the groups used in the programme). Pupils discuss and adjust their targets on a weekly basis as part of the group. It has proved very effective with primary pupils in a transfer group to spend time talking about their likes and dislikes, what they are excited about in terms of the transfer, what they are worried about, what they think is going to be most difficult, etc. The aim is to develop the opportunity for peer support and the recognition that their worries are quite common. Building group strategies for dealing with new situations is very helpful, as are specific strategies to help pupils with their identified areas of weakness. If pupils are going to the same secondary school there is the added advantage that they have already identified a supportive peer or group.

Secondary school visits

Secondary school visits are very important. However, many Year 6 pupils visiting their secondary school will do so on a specially arranged day when either most pupils are not on site or a specially arranged curriculum is on offer to minimise disruption. While this means Year 6 visitors are not immediately put off, the first day of the September term, when 'normal' operations are in force, can come as a bit of a shock. For pupils who are likely to find this transfer more difficult, additional visits are very helpful. As far as the transfer process is concerned, the conversations after secondary visits are important. Generally pupils are excited and reassured by their visits but any concerns can be discussed further and sometimes specific ideas for support can be formulated at this point. For example, a pupil who found it impossible to follow the timetable and map on a visit is going to need some extra support in the first week or so. The extra support can often be easily identified as a role for another pupil or for a sixth form mentor. Most secondary schools will have strategies for helping pupils settle in – it is a case of utilising them before problems develop.

Information sharing with parents/carers

It is important that information sharing with parents/carers is built in to any strategy you try. The importance of parental support and parents/carers feeling supported cannot be emphasised too much. It is preferable for parents/carers to keep in touch on a regular basis with the work being undertaken to prepare pupils for transfer. If parents/carers are not in regular contact with the school it is useful to arrange a specific meeting time when information can be given as the process progresses and at which queries or concerns can be raised. Meetings at school can be daunting or difficult to attend and there may be instances where the use of a learning mentor or a phone call home may be one way of keeping everyone informed. It is also important that parents are given the opportunity to share information with professionals. Pupils may share feelings and fears at home that they feel they cannot share at school.

Stages of the transfer process – at secondary school

Group work continues

When the pupil starts at secondary school the group work continues as support for pupils after transfer. In the primary/secondary transfer project we tried to use the same member of the team to support a pupil after transfer. Where this was not possible we ensured that the original adult that the pupil had worked with did visit them in secondary school to facilitate a handover process.

Group work in secondary schools was run with a member of the school staff in the majority of cases, the aim being to hand over the support of this pupil to the secondary school's pastoral system. Where the process is being assisted by support staff from outside the school they may facilitate this transfer and handover process. If the process is being coordinated by the schools themselves (which is always the ultimate aim), then key staff from the primary and secondary schools will need to have planned this stage. Some schools allocate senior teachers to the role of liaison with primary schools. In other schools this role may be fulfilled by the learning mentors. Whatever link is used the pupils will need to be aware that communication has taken place and that their identified needs are being considered and appropriate support put in place. As far as confidentiality is concerned, information shared in group sessions is only passed on with the permission of the pupil. They may take a while to get used to a new adult in this supportive role and they need to feel comfortable and safe that confidences are only shared at their request.

Targets set and monitored

The basis for the group work continues to be monitoring and reviewing of targets. It also offers pupils the opportunity to express and discuss issues and concerns in a confidential and supportive environment. If there are specific issues which need further work, such as bullying or truanting, the group leader may decide to use available resources to do a specific input on the issue within the group work framework. Resources for group work were listed at the end of Chapter 4. The group takes place on a weekly basis if possible, with the same format as pre-transfer work. The majority of pupils offered the group work reported that they felt supported and valued the weekly discussions and peer support.

Referral to other appropriate in-school support

Ideally group work is run by secondary school staff or LEA support services with secondary school staff, the aim being to support the transition and assist the secondary school with identifying which internal support systems will be applicable. For some pupils the attendance at a weekly meeting for the first term or half a term is sufficient to offer support at a difficult time and until it is apparent that they are doing well. For others it may highlight a concern; for example, attendance that can be referred on to the relevant supporting agency. In the example used of attendance it may be that at the school's premises the Educational Welfare Officer runs groups or offers support for pupils with attendance problems and that referring the pupil to this support is the most appropriate way forward. It may be that referral to the learning mentor for more individual support is considered helpful.

Case Study 5.1

Accessing appropriate support

Identified by primary school

Ben was highlighted by his primary school as needing support in the transition phase to secondary school because of his emotional and behavioural difficulties. He had experienced problems at primary school and in Year 6 was transferred from one class into the parallel class midway through the year to be with a very experienced teacher.

CISS and target setting

Ben was very happy to participate in assessing himself using the CISS. He asked if he could rate himself as he was behaving in his new class as he felt this was going better than the rest of the year had gone. We agreed together that this was fine and also agreed to note on the CISS that this is what we were doing. Ben's rating of himself was consequently relatively high, although he was very honest in admitting this was very recent positive behaviour. This left an opportunity to talk about situations he had found difficult in the past. (One of the advantages of using the CISS with pupils is that you are thinking together about numerous situations and issues and the majority of pupils engage in discussing these with a very positive attitude.) We were able to set some clear and realistic targets from his ratings. One of these targets was about his response to the comments of a pair of pupils who sat at the same table with him. He reported that they frequently, at least every day, told him how he should sit on his chair, e.g. not leaning back on two legs, not leaning over the desk. He said he was unable to resist responding and this did get him in to trouble. We talked about various ways he could deal with the situation. He felt strongly that they should mind their own business and that he would find it difficult to completely ignore them as a consequence. We decided together on a strategy that he was very keen to try. He would try to do something they did not expect. He would smile at them and sit properly on his chair. This way he felt he was allowed to respond but in a way that might not encourage further interference from the protagonists.

Group work

Ben joined a small group of pupils preparing for the secondary transfer who had rated themselves and set targets in a similar manner. When he came along to the first group session he was eager to share the results of his new strategy. It had been a great success and he had enjoyed responding in an unexpected way. Ben enjoyed the group work sessions and was encouraged to find another group member was going to the same secondary school. They developed a supportive relationship whereas previously they had only been aware of each other.

At secondary school

Ben continued with small group work once a week at secondary school. He was experiencing some problems but the project worker assisted the secondary Head of Year in identifying appropriate support. He was assigned a learning mentor early in Year 7. This meant that as the group work came to an end he could continue being supported by someone he had developed a relationship with over the first term. The secondary school was also able to use internal communication systems to indicate to subject teachers the areas of possible concern so that if problems arose teachers felt informed and empowered with strategies. The project worker was consulted and offered advice on problems as they arose and the school staff felt supported and valued for the efforts they were making to include Ben in all aspect of school life.

Conclusions

Ben was a pupil able to gain valuable strategies and support by using the CISS and participating in the group work process. He felt supported both before and after moving to secondary school.

The primary school was able to offer additional information to the secondary school and to assist in offering Ben additional pre-transfer support.

The secondary school was able to plan more effectively for Ben because it had more information initially, developed a supportive relationship with Ben through the group work and gained the support and suggestions of the project worker.

Results of initial pilot in Wandsworth

In the pilot of the primary/secondary transfer project in Wandsworth 49 primary pupils were offered pre-transfer support at the request of their primary schools. (An example of the evaluation framework used can be found in Appendix 6.) Thirteen of the pupils went to out-of-borough schools and were more difficult to track. Out-of-borough secondary schools were contacted, a key person identified and information sent on in the form of CISS scales and summary information on a pro-forma (Appendix 7). Of the 36 pupils who remained in Wandsworth schools all were offered support and all were successful in their initial transfer. Secondary schools were generally very supportive of the initiative and used the information and group work feedback to plan appropriately for individual pupils. Those pupils who needed additional support appeared to be receiving this by the end of the first term, which would seem to suggest they had accessed support more quickly than they would have done without the transfer process being initiated. All pupils had been fully transferred to the secondary school support systems by the end of the first term. They continue to be monitored.

One secondary school initiated a different approach to deal with a group of pupils identified as needing extra support.

Year 7 supported group

In one secondary school a group of Year 7 pupils had been set up to include pupils identified by their primary schools as at risk of not making a successful transfer to a secondary school because of their emotional and behavioural needs. The members of the senior management team and the tutor of the group felt enabled to offer a different approach for this group of pupils because they knew they would be receiving the support and guidance of the project team. This was a smaller group (12 pupils) than the other tutor groups in the school. The pupils received a full curriculum but their timetable had been carefully planned to avoid changing rooms unless necessary. They had a base room where the majority of their lessons took place. They moved for specialist subjects like science or art where the equipment is all in one place. They had a Learning Support Assistant with the class in all lessons.

All the pupils had been assessed in retrospect by the primary feeder schools and by themselves on the CISS. This information has been used to inform the approaches staff at secondary school took and for the setting of individual targets. A re-integration group took place for those pupils who were ready to move back into a 'mainstream' tutor group. Group approaches were used to help them develop strategies for successful integration. It was a very challenging group of pupils and staff adopted differentiated approaches to dealing with them. Staff had input from the Inclusion Pilot Project team who helped them develop strategies for use with these pupils. There were several children in this group who would not have remained in school without this adapted approach. The case study that follows originally appeared in *This time I'll stay: Re-integrating young people permanently excluded from school: Approaches to effective practice from schools and Local Education Authorities* published by Include.

Case Study 5.2

Application of 'The Coping in Schools Programme'

Background

The school where the intervention strategy was used was a mixed secondary school with a five-form entry.

In previous years the secondary school had offered additional support to a group of Year 7 pupils highlighted for their learning needs by the primary schools.

This year a different group was highlighted. The target group comprised pupils transferring from primary schools where the primary feeder schools had expressed concerns about the pupils' ability to cope with the transfer due to the nature of their emotional and behavioural difficulties.

There were 12 pupils in this target group with six coming from one primary school and the others all coming from separate schools.

Approach

The approach involved four stages.

1. Communication of the programme and methods through training

At this school initial communication took place with the senior management team. The whole of the staff group then received training on an INSET day that looked at the *Social Inclusion: Pupil Support* guidance (in draft form at that stage) and how this approach would fit within this framework.

2. Assessment

The school decided to use the programme to support the integration of 12 pupils identified by the primary schools as having emotional and behavioural difficulties. Primary feeder schools were asked to complete an assessment using the Coping in Schools Scale (CISS). The target pupils were also asked to complete a self-assessment using the same scale. This self-assessment by the pupils allows a comparison of pupils' and teachers' perceptions of the problem. It also establishes a dialogue with the pupil and identifies specific problem areas.

3. Development of intervention programmes

The pupils followed a full curriculum but a base room was established and subject teachers came to them, except for specialist subjects where specific room-based equipment was needed. This, therefore, kept movement around the school to a minimum for this group. The group was double staffed at all times and allocated experienced and high profile teachers for the majority of subjects.

The project team (consultant, EP and teacher) observed the class across the whole day, on a number of occasions noting successful strategies used, problem areas, times of the day that were particularly problematic, etc.

Feedback from these observations and from the CISS scores was disseminated to all teaching staff of the group in a number of twilight sessions. These sessions also offered teachers the opportunity to discuss problems and successes with each other and share strategies for use with this difficult group of pupils. The project team managed these sessions.

Within this framework it was also decided which pupils would begin the process of re-integration back into the mainstream groups first.

The pupils' assessment was used as a starting point for target setting. Feedback and information from ratings and observations to all teachers of the group enabled positive strategies to be developed for the management of this group.

From this, simple reward systems were developed for the pupils.

There were two elements to the feedback: (a) staff development and (b) specific pupil needs.

4. Implementation and monitoring

The staff agreed and applied specific strategies and observed the effectiveness of these. Pupils' targets were monitored and changed if necessary on a weekly basis. Regular meetings offered the whole staff group the opportunity to monitor and change approaches used to the needs of the pupils, therefore developing their own skills also. Where strategies proved ineffective further change was implemented; for example, one specialist subject was changed to being taught in the base room.

Consequences

Early re-integration

By the beginning of the second term two of the original 12 pupils had been re-integrated full time into other Year 7 groups and a further seven were re-integrating on a part-time basis.

As a result of the close observation and monitoring of the group, two of the pupils had their medication dosage and timing changed and were among the first to re-integrate.

Staff development

Staff reported that the intervention programme and advice from the team supported their professional development.

There was a general positive shift in perceptions of staff with regard to the pupils throughout the process.

Setting up transfer support: summary of important issues

- Who will offer the support? Where? When?
- Parental perceptions and support.
- Pupils' views and concerns.
- Links between primary and secondary school.
- Pupil visits to secondary school.
- Information needed by the receiving school.
- Post-transfer support. Who? Where? When?
- Support systems and how to access them.
- How support and information is communicated to all staff in the secondary school who work with this pupil.
- Is there a role for other agencies?

Key points

➤ It is important to reflect on the complete nature of the transfer that we ask pupils to make between primary and secondary school.

➤ The supportive transfer process outlined had communication as a key element.

➤ Parents are fully involved in the process.

➤ There is two-way reciprocal information sharing between parents and professionals.

➤ Baseline information on behavioural needs is assessed using the CISS.

> ➤ Pupils rate themselves and set their own targets.
> ➤ Pupils receive pre-transfer support to assist them in preparing for secondary transition.
> ➤ Pupils receive post-transfer support with a group work approach.
> ➤ Secondary schools are helped through the process to initiate appropriate support for pupils as they transfer.
> ➤ An example of an alternative approach to transfer for a small group of vulnerable pupils is explored.

Food for thought

In order to understand children fully we must study the inter-relations among the social, cognitive and affective aspects of their behaviour and development. For example, if we were interested in studying what is typically considered a dimension of cognition, reading, we should be concerned with cognitive linguistic processes (such as knowledge of letter-sound correspondence), social processes (such as the ways in which children's knowledge of the social conventions govern classroom discourse), and affect (such as achievement motivation). Similarly, in studying children's social behaviour, such as cooperation with peers, we must consider cognitive processes, such as the ability to take another person's perspective. The reason for the examination of social, affective and cognitive processes is simple: they affect each other.

(Pellegrini and Blatchford 2000)

We are often much more effective in planning for the learning needs of pupils on transfer than we are at planning for their social and emotional needs. A pupil who has found it difficult to make relationships with adults and peers at primary school will find the transfer to secondary school a daunting process, as we have discussed in this chapter. One case study example was given of a secondary school that had put in place a different strategy for vulnerable pupils at transfer.

Questions

How might you plan for the needs of pupils with social, emotional and behavioural difficulties either pre- or post-transfer?

How might you foster links with schools of the other phase (primary or secondary) to promote more supportive transfer for these pupils?

How might you promote a whole-school approach to supporting this group of pupils in Year 7?

Chapter 6

Learning Support Units

Questions this chapter aims to answer
What are the features of a successful in-school centre?
What information needs to be shared about pupils to make the support in the LSU most successful?
How might support systems in the school need to be adapted to assist re-integration from the LSU?
What issues might need to be considered to facilitate the working of units with linked schools?
What is the role of steering groups and why are they valuable?
How are clear referral procedures implemented?
How are pupils involved in the process?

Early intervention	Learning Support Unit	Pastoral Support Programme	Pupil Referral Unit
Coping in School Scale (CISS) and programme	Referral process Coping in School Scale (CISS)	Systematic assessment Coping in School Scale (CISS)	Re-integration programme Re-integration Readiness Scale (RRS)
	Intervention programme	Target setting	Group work
Code of Practice (COP) Stage 2 (New COP School Action)	Code of Practice (COP) Stage 3 (New COP School Action Plus)	Code of Practice (COP) Stage 3 (New COP School Action Plus)	

Re-integration	Re-integration	Re-integration
SUPPORT		

Figure 6.1 A continuum of support for pupils with emotional and behavioural difficulties

Having looked in the previous chapter at strategies for early intervention for pupils transferring to secondary school we now need to consider the role of the Learning Support Unit in the continuum for pupils with emotional and behavioural difficulties.

Learning Support Units (LSUs), or in-school centres as they are sometimes referred to, are not a new idea but recent funding has placed LSUs firmly back in the centre of in-school provision for pupils with challenging behaviour. The access of all inner city schools to an LSU is stated in the Excellence in Cities initiative (DfEE 1999a) and expanded in more detail in the *Social Inclusion: Pupil Support* guidance, Circular 10/99 (DfEE 1999b). An LSU provides short-term teaching and support tailored to the needs of identified pupils. It is designed to be a positive preventive strategy and should have clear entry and exit criteria. Entry to the unit should be planned, short term, and with an emphasis on helping pupils develop strategies to manage in a mainstream classroom. It is therefore important that re-integration is always a key element and carefully planned and supported. Although offering a different approach and curriculum, the LSU should be firmly embedded in the school and accepted as part of that school culture. It is on the same site (except for link schools for shared units); pupils wear the same uniform and generally spend part of the day or week in their mainstream lessons in the same building. Some schools have access to a unit in another school and where this is the case careful liaison and regular communication is essential. Initially secondary schools were targeted for implementation of the LSU initiative but now increasing numbers of primary schools have access to an LSU. The model described and issues raised apply equally well to units in both the primary and secondary phases.

After some of the sections in this chapter a set of questions is provided that may be useful as guidelines to managers, steering groups or working parties. These are questions that will need answering when setting up a new system (the Learning Support Unit) that needs to be embedded within a whole-school approach. There are specific questions relating to the setting up of linked units (units based in one school but offering support for one or more other schools).

Success factors

There are many different models of successful in-school centres in terms of how they run on a day-to-day basis but there appears to be a number of factors which contribute to the success of whichever model is adopted:

- the active involvement of senior staff, teachers and parents;
- good communication within the school;
- using an approach which combines the withdrawal of pupils and support for them within normal classes;
- flexibility in the provision of support;
- the involvement of the pupils in self-monitoring

(Hallam and Castle 1999)

In the *Evaluation of the Behaviour and Discipline Pilot Projects (1996–99) Supported under the Standards Fund Programme* (Hallam and Castle 1999) examples of good practice were cited such as the clear assessment of problems, identification and prioritising of needs, and involving pupils in target setting. Using the Coping in Schools Scale and programme can assist with meeting the above criteria.

Before looking in more detail at stages of the process of using an LSU it would be worth raising some more general issues that may need to be discussed with the staff group in the school. To introduce and maintain an initiative such as an in-school centre, and to ensure its success, thought needs to be given to how it will dovetail with existing in-school provision. How will information be shared and what information is needed? What support networks are needed for staff and pupils and how will these be enhanced? What changes will need to be made to existing systems and how will this be effected? How will existing LEA support services complement this provision?

Information, support and systems

Information

In order to effectively tailor a programme to an individual pupil's needs it is essential that all the information that will facilitate that process is available. At each of the stages in the process detailed below it is necessary to bear in mind the importance of information for planning, consolidating progress and further development. There are questions that need to be asked in relation to the giving and receiving of information. These questions apply to the range of adults involved with the pupil, such as subject teachers, tutors, LSU managers, Heads of Year and learning mentors.

After coming up with ideas for important areas of information that need to be shared, the next hurdle is how will this be shared in a meaningful and manageable way? How the dissemination of information is structured will depend on the way your school works and the way you feel information is most effectively shared within this system. One thing that seems best to avoid is generating lots of additional paperwork that nobody will read. Some schools have staff notice boards that are well used but this will only be appropriate for certain kinds of information. In some schools pupils have their own diaries that they keep with them at all times and it may be appropriate for targets to be recorded in these. One issue for all Learning Support Units is the gathering and sharing of information and once this system is developed everything becomes much easier.

Strategies that have been shown to work include:

- developing a systematic and consistent referral process so that everyone is clear what is needed and by when it is needed;
- LSU managers participating regularly at various team meetings (departmental, year, learning support) in the secondary school and being provided with a clear slot for communication at primary staff meetings;
- a member of the SMT being actively involved in the planning and overview of how the LSU functions, and supporting that process.

There are various sorts of information that might be useful. The following examples were distilled from discussion with colleagues.

Basic information
Literacy, numeracy skills, reading skills, outside agencies involved, medical needs, disabilities, whether the pupil is a child looked after by the local authority (CLA) or is on the Child Protection Register, key worker.

Expectations
Targets the pupil is working on, aims of re-integration, strategies used to help pupil, strategies pupil is trying to use, positive efforts pupil is making.

Practical guidelines
Where they should sit, whom they should be separated from, potential triggers, fears.

What they have been working on
What support they have received in the LSU, how that has worked.

Questions relating to the effective sharing of information

What information do you need?
How might this information best be passed on to you to ensure you take note of it?
What information will you feed back and to whom about the pupil?
How will this be organised?

Support

Support for pupils, teachers, LSU managers and parents should be built into each stage of the process. If the LSU is firmly embedded within the school's ethos and pastoral support systems then managing the support of all those involved becomes easier. This is not the case if the LSU is seen as an add-on. There are a number of important questions to ask that again apply to a range of adults working with the pupil.

Support for staff
Feedback from teachers both in units and in classrooms indicates a number of suggestions for the effective support for staff:

- support for receiving teachers can take place in the classroom;
- support could be offered for a whole department via meeting time or INSET;
- classroom teachers need to know what to do and whom to contact for support if things are not running smoothly;
- there needs to be contingency for immediate support and for raising more general concerns;
- learning mentors may be used to support this process if they are available in your school.

Whatever the support process is, it is important that everyone understands and is clear about the ground rules and the key personnel involved.

Support for pupils

Pupils need to be clear what support is available and how to access it. Support within the LSU will probably be easier to manage than support when they are in mainstream lessons. There need to be clear guidelines for pupils on what to do if they feel things are not going well. There also needs to be regular monitoring of how individual pupils are using the support offered. Pupils may have accessed the learning mentor either individually or within a group prior to the LSU as an early intervention strategy. Thought needs to be given to whether that relationship and support continues and in what form while the pupil is also using the LSU. The pupils will need to be involved in deciding what support they find valuable and how many different people they want to be involved.

Questions relating to the planning of effective support

What support might you need for re-integrating the pupil?
From whom do you require this support?
What support is already in place for the pupil and how might this be best utilised?
What changes do you plan to make to this process?
Who needs to be kept informed and how?
Does the pupil feel in control of the transition?
What does the pupil think he or she needs?

Systems

The existing systems need to be closely analysed to ensure that the process of referral to, use of, and re-integration from the LSU is firmly embedded in good practice in the school.

Setting up a steering group or working party, which needs to meet regularly, is one way of ensuring all these elements are considered. The formation of such a group can be very supportive to the LSU manager as well as offering the opportunity for wider staff groups to be involved in the development and evaluation of the provision. In terms of implementing the good practice found in the evaluative research of the Improving Behaviour Projects (Hallam and Castle 1999), it helps to facilitate the active involvement of senior staff and other teachers and also assists in the process of communication and collaboration.

> **Questions relating to adaptation of existing systems**
>
> What systems could be adapted, enhanced or put in place to facilitate and implement the information transfer?
> What systems could be adapted, enhanced or put in place to facilitate and implement the support and full re-integration of pupils?
> Who will need to be involved in any changes suggested?
> How will the effectiveness of changes be monitored?
> Who will do the monitoring?

Linked units

It is worth briefly highlighting some additional issues for units which although based in one school also offer support for one or more other schools. Many of the primary LSUs are set up on this basis and some secondary units also. In many respects the idea of a unit shared between several schools has advantages. The development of supportive communities around groups of schools offers a wealth of opportunities for sharing expertise and resources to meet the needs of individual pupils. In practice, the process of setting up a shared unit needs to be well managed and time and effort need to go into maintaining communication and a shared ethos for the running of the unit and the support it offers pupils. The steering group for these units (see pages 69–70) is often a pivotal element of this communication framework.

Setting up the unit

All the school partners need to consult about and agree: the structure of access to the unit; an overview of the curriculum offered; referral procedures; reporting guidelines. The same approach should be adopted towards other issues. Although it is unlikely that all aspects of the provision will be 'right first time', if all involved are in agreement initially then agreeing changes later will be easier. If each school is to have a different amount of access this should be agreed in the initial stages and regularly reviewed. Opportunities for staff from partner schools to visit the unit both before and after it starts to function are a useful way of making everyone feel part of the project. The professional relationship between the manager and the other staff in the unit is an essential element in developing policy and delivering practice. It is important that all staff feel informed about partner schools.

Referral procedures

These need to be agreed by all parties but the LSU manager will need to think through what information he or she will need to work with pupils from a different school. In the first instance, visits to the partner schools will be essential for LSU managers to familiarise themselves with differences in expectations, routines and procedures of the partner schools. The target setting and strategies worked on with pupils will be informed by these visits.

If it is possible for observation of referred pupils to take place then useful insights can be gained by staff from the LSU. It is also helpful if LSU staff can meet with pupils in their own schools at some point prior to the placement. This helps to make clear links for the pupil.

Logistics

It is important to clarify for all concerned how pupils are going to get to and from the unit. If access is for full days this may be less problematic but many units may offer sessions. These problems are not insurmountable but careful thought at the outset can prevent worries later. It is important that all pupils attending the unit are receiving the same kind of programme and that there are not disparities for linked schools.

Times of the school day and procedures for break and lunch-time in each partner school will need to be clarified. If the timings in the LSU are to be different this will need to be agreed.

Uniform is also an issue to consider. In most units the pupils will continue to wear the uniform of their own schools but this needs to be agreed.

Questions that will need answering when setting up a system

How might the day be structured to offer the best support in the most practical way for pupils from all schools in the partnership? If, for example, half-day sessions are decided to be most appropriate for pupils, how are they going to get to and from the unit?

Are there going to be separate start and finish times to enable pupils from other schools to arrive for the start of the session?

How will break and lunch times be managed for pupils from other schools?

What uniform will be worn?

Working with parents

Working with parents needs to be carefully considered. Parents may be more tentative about their child spending time in the LSU if it is based in another school. The management of pupils attending two different sites and pupils' individual needs should be planned and parents need to visit the LSU and be clear about the logistics of, for example, how their child will get to the unit and back if this is on a sessional basis (see above).

> **Questions that will need answering when setting up a system**
>
> How will you approach parents about the LSU placement?
> How will visits to the unit be organised?
> Are there likely to be transport issues and how could these be overcome?
> Who will be the key link person for communicating with parents once the pupil is at the unit?

Discipline policy and procedures

Discipline procedures need to be agreed by all the schools involved. Acceptable codes of behaviour for the unit should be clarified and would generally follow the school's behaviour policy. In this instance we have policies of several schools and while it is unlikely that they will be vastly different clarity needs to be sought. In addition it is worth having a clear procedure about what will happen in the event of a pupil exhibiting unacceptable behaviour in either setting. Communication about incidents needs to be rapid and clear.

> **Questions that will need answering when setting up a system**
>
> Is there an agreed code of behaviour for the LSU?
> If incidents occur, who is the key person to contact in either setting?
> If the pupil is excluded for a fixed term from either setting, how will that affect the other placement?
> Are there proactive plans in place for emergencies?
> Who will inform the parents?

Reporting on intervention

At the end of the placement in the LSU (and sometimes at intervals during a placement) the manager will write a report detailing the provision and how the pupil has accessed the curriculum, responded to strategies offered, interacted with peers, etc. It is worth agreeing a format that satisfies everyone. Repetition of administrative work can be avoided. It may also be possible to link this reporting with reviews of the pupils' IEPs.

> **Questions that will need answering when setting up a system**
>
> Is there an agreed pro-forma for reporting on a pupil's progress?
> Is there agreement on the frequency of reporting?
> Can reporting be linked with reviewing the pupil's IEP?

Ongoing support

Pupils accessing an LSU will require ongoing support of some sort for varying periods of time. Some outreach work in linked schools is a valuable way of ensuring that there is continuity of support for the pupil. It also ensures a proper handover of the support to in-school systems.

Questions that will need answering when setting up a system

What support will be offered to pupils when they re-integrate from the LSU?
Who will offer this support and for how long?
How will the support be linked to in-school support systems?
Who will monitor this support?

The following guidelines are taken from aspects of positive and supportive steering groups for LSUs. Each steering group will need to develop according to the needs of the particular school or partnership of schools that it serves. Obviously steering groups for units with linking schools will have different agenda items and communication issues from a unit that only takes pupils from the school in which it is based.

Steering groups

Purposes

The purpose of a steering group is to support and promote the work of the LSU within the school or group of linked schools in which it is based. Part of its brief is to take a strategic overview for planning changes to the provision offered by the LSU when this is needed. Another element is evaluating outcomes for pupils who have accessed LSU provision so that good practice can be built upon.

The steering group will have a number of issues to consider, including:

- promoting a positive image of the LSU;
- communication with the rest of the school and with linked schools where applicable;
- the curriculum offered within the LSU and any changes needed to this in the light of experience;
- the re-integration of pupils from the LSU, support needed and received;
- links with other in-school support systems, i.e. learning mentors, pastoral teams;
- links with outside agencies and how these can be developed;
- communication with parents.

Staff involved in the steering group

The steering group needs to involve a member of the senior management team, the LSU manager, learning mentors (or a representative) and Heads of Year (or at least one representative for secondary schools). It is also advisable to enlist some outside support and advice at these meetings to add additional perspectives; this may be an LEA representative (Behaviour Support Team, Educational Psychologist or other relevant person). An LEA coordinator could be involved in LSU steering groups across all the participating schools. This has proved to be a very effective means of disseminating good practice in each LSU to all the others. Inevitably different schools employ different strategies and we can all learn from the successful practice of others as well as from their mistakes. Having input from someone from the LEA who attends a number of different steering groups is an effective method of support and of developing links between schools.

Reporting guidelines

The DfEE have issued extensive guidelines on what they require in terms of reporting back on LSUs. To assist schools in meeting the reporting requirements it is useful to keep up-to-date records of the sort of information required. Some of this is school-based information on social inclusion performance indicators such as:

- reduction in the number of pupils on fixed-term exclusions;
- reduction in the number of permanently excluded pupils;
- an increase in the number of pupils re-integrated from the PRU.

Some of the information requirements are specific to the LSU such as:

- the total number of pupils accessing the LSU;
- a breakdown of length of time the pupils spent in the unit;
- the pattern of attendance at the unit;
- evidence of improved behavioural attainments in relation to baseline assessment.

If the LSU manager reports back on these targets (and the others listed in the guidance) on a regular basis to the steering group then any reports required by the LEA or DfEE are easily put together with up-to-date information.

Accessing the Learning Support Unit

> **Stages of the process**
>
> Referral procedures.
> Pupil self-assessment and target setting.
> Planning for individual needs.
> Time in the unit and supported time in class.
> Full re-integration and post-re-integration support.
> Evaluation of the support offered.

Referral procedures

Secondary schools

It is important that a clear referral procedure to the Learning Support Unit is agreed. Ideally this procedure is agreed prior to the establishment of the unit and can be developed through a steering group or working party. In some secondary schools this referral is through the Heads of Year, who may be part of an ongoing steering group. Pupils will usually be referred to the Head of Year for persistent problems or concerns by their tutor or a subject department. Most schools have existing systems for referring behaviour problems in stages to the appropriate member of staff. For example, this may include:

1. Initial problems dealt with by class teacher.
2. Referral to department head if problems are repeated.
3. Referral to Head of Year for problems unable to be dealt with within the department.

It varies from school to school at which stages parents are informed and also whether tutors are informed of actions taken at each stage.

Ideally pupils are offered support and guidance at these earlier stages to try to prevent the problem developing or being compounded. Within the Coping in Schools programme small group work could be offered at an early stage of concern, with target setting and peer support being part of the programme, as discussed in earlier chapters (see Chapters 4 and 5).

If the Head of Year is concerned about problems and believes that the pupil may need a higher level of support than is being offered at an early intervention stage, he or she may consider the Learning Support Unit would offer this more intensive level of support and intervention.

Heads of Year may bring their referrals to a steering group or in some schools the referrals take place at a separate meeting.

Primary schools

The referral procedure in primary schools is usually through consultation with the SENCO and class teacher.

Primary and Secondary schools

Wherever the referral procedure takes place consideration needs to be given to a number of factors when deciding on groupings. The balance of pupils in the unit will depend on the dynamics of the school, unit and pupils, so there can be no formula that works in all cases. Often this balance is developed over time and through experience and the manager will need the support of other staff (through the steering group) to achieve and maintain the best balance possible. It is almost completely pointless to select the most troubled children in the school and put them together for extended periods of time and expect a quick, successful outcome. The aim of any pupil's placement in a Learning Support Unit must be that some beneficial outcome will be achieved. It may not always be possible but it should be a realistic aim.

Consideration needs to be given to all of the following when trying to balance a group:

- Do the pupils we are proposing to group together already have a negative history with each other?
- Are we able to achieve a balance of acting-out and withdrawn pupils? How will these pupils manage together?
- Is there a balance of gender placements (if this is appropriate)?
- Is there a mixture of year groups? Is this useful?
- Are there pupils within the group who need extra help with basic literacy and numeracy? Can peer support be promoted?

When a placement has been decided there needs to be clarity on the proposed time-scale of the intervention and how re-integration will be promoted and supported. These issues will be discussed in more detail below.

At this stage the manager will need detailed information about the pupils who are to be placed in the unit. LSU managers can gather this information from teaching staff, support staff, parents and the pupils themselves. A detailed profile of the pupil's academic, learning, emotional and behavioural needs is helpful to this process. Access to academic records and National Curriculum levels should be fairly straightforward. Accessing behavioural strengths and weaknesses may be more complicated. Many schools have well-established procedures for recording incidents that will be helpful as part of the profile. It is also important to assess general behaviour in the classroom and to ensure that strengths as well as weaknesses are highlighted. Using the CISS as a baseline for behaviour across subject areas is a clear and consistent way of collecting this information. It is important that as complete a profile as possible is used. In primary schools this will probably involve asking the class teacher, any support staff, and possibly the Head Teacher or SENCO (if they have detailed knowledge of the pupil) to complete the full version of the CISS. In secondary schools the tutor or Head of Year would complete the full version and all subject teachers would be asked to complete the shorter version of the CISS. It is particularly important in secondary schools that information is gathered across subject areas as the pupil may behave differently with different teachers or across different types of subjects. For example, the pupil may find more structured academic subjects (e.g. Maths, English, History) easier to manage than subjects that are less structured and demand more self-control or self-management (e.g. Drama and Music). It could of course prove to be the other way round.

The Coping in Schools Scale is a valuable tool for a number of purposes at this stage. As detailed in Chapter 4, using the CISS provides a range of information across subjects and enables comparison of teacher and pupil perceptions. The data will assist with setting targets, deciding in a structured way which subjects can be maintained throughout the LSU placement and which order to re-integrate to other subjects. They will offer a clear indication of those subjects which will require the most support during re-integration and will also offer a baseline from which progress can be measured and the effectiveness of the intervention can be assessed. The following case study illustrates the procedure one primary LSU manager has initiated for collecting data using the CISS.

Case Study 6.1

Granard Primary School Learning Support Unit

Background

The Coping in Schools Scale (CISS) has been utilised by Granard Learning Support Unit to assess the individual needs of children who might be included within the LSU. The prerequisite for inclusion within the LSU is an initial identification by the school SENCO in consultation with individual class teachers. All children identified require intervention at Stage 3 of the Code of Practice.

Implementation

The CISS was given initially to the child's individual class teacher to complete. Each teacher was asked to complete only the sections requiring assessment of questions on the 1 to 4 scale, and to disregard the comments section. A subsequent interview between the class teacher and the LSU teacher took place, whereby the comments section was completed with the class teacher giving an oral response to each section. It was felt that this might elicit a more accurate reflection of children's particular needs as seen by their teachers.

Once the CISS had been completed, and the data analysed by the LSU teacher, the children were interviewed using the CISS. The children were free to add any comments in the relevant sections during the interview.

The two sets of CISS were further analysed by the LSU teacher to identify possible areas of agreement between pupil and teacher, or indeed to identify any disparity.

Findings

Feedback from teachers indicated their overall ease with completion of the CISS. The 'interview' with the teacher provided much specific information, which took into consideration some of the inconsistencies of exhibited behaviour that may have been omitted otherwise.

The children found the CISS to be quite comprehensive and a rather lengthy process; in some cases the children were taking up to 40 minutes to complete the task. It was felt that given the age of the children they could cope with this amount of time on a single task. However, towards the end of the session they were becoming weary. Consequently, breaking this time into two shorter sessions, as recommended, may prove of greater benefit.

The CISS proved to be a most valuable tool in assessing the individual needs of the children in question. It provided a wealth of detail in a child-centred, positive way. The CISS concentrated on the strengths of the children, allowing a clear focus to develop for areas of further development. A clear appreciation of where the children were at emerged, facilitating a realistic approach to target setting.

Pupil self-assessment and target setting

It is vital that the pupil is central to the process of planning and target setting for access to the LSU.

As described in Chapter 4, it is important that pupils assess themselves using the CISS and set their own targets so that they have ownership of the process and their role in the planned intervention. Pupils offered this opportunity often voice their appreciation of being included in the planning. It is important that the pupil continues to be involved in monitoring and reviewing targets and planning for support. For further details on how to use the CISS with pupils, refer to Chapter 4.

Planning for individual needs

Following completion of the CISS as part of the referral procedure, re-integration to classes can be planned in a structured way. If there are lessons that are clearly working and causing minimal problems it is important that attendance at these lessons is maintained throughout the time in the unit. Conversely, lessons where there are clear indications of problems may need careful planning before effective re-integration can take place. There may be lessons where support is needed and where a change of group or teacher could be considered. There may be specific issues around accessing the curriculum in some lessons and additional input in this curriculum area may be planned for the pupil while they are in the unit. As part of the individual planning undertaken it will be important to look at the match between teacher and pupil perceptions and address any issues raised by this in a supportive and constructive way.

Whether there is a discernible pattern or not, looking at strengths and weaknesses will help planning for the pupil.

Time in the unit and in mainstream classes

For pupils who are able to receive support in the unit it is an ideal opportunity to develop social and group work skills. Many of the pupils referred to the unit will experience problems relating to other people, both peers and adults, and the potential for the development of social skills is clear. Many pupils may also need help with basic skills and this is an ideal opportunity to offer such support. If pupils are also attending some mainstream lessons (and ideally this should be the case throughout the time in the unit) they can receive support, encouragement and the opportunity to discuss strategies and problems before and after attending lessons. It is essential that they see the staff in the Learning Support Unit as supportive adults and that they can develop relationships with these adults.

Full re-integration and post-re-integration support

If the full re-integration back into the mainstream is not planned and supported this is often the point at which all the good work put in by staff and pupils comes apart. Many pupils do very well while in the Learning Support Unit. They thrive in a smaller group and can find it quite difficult to cope with the full timetable. However, problems can be averted or minimised if the transition is supported well. It is not possible for the manager or even other staff in a larger unit to offer all the support needed to all the pupils. It is so important that the unit and its work is embedded in the school and is part of what the school as a whole has to offer. All staff will need to be part of the support offered to pupils, to help them monitor and maintain their targets and encourage their progress. Pupils re-integrating will certainly need a key person with whom they can discuss their targets. Many may benefit from a continuation of group work with peers on a weekly basis. It may be that they return to the level of support offered under the early intervention model in Chapter 4.

Some pupils will have felt much happier working with a small group in a supportive environment and they may not want to fully re-integrate to mainstream lessons. You need to have clear strategies to deal with this problem. The LSU is intended to be used as a short-term input. Pupils need to be fully aware from the outset that the time in the unit is limited. Re-integration needs to be built into the programme from the beginning and it is advisable for all pupils to be attending some mainstream lessons while they are attending the LSU. It is clear that pupils will need to have some ongoing support and using the full range of the school's pastoral support system is important.

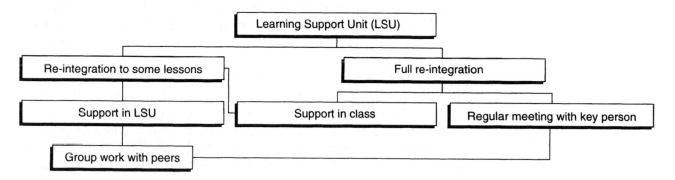

Figure 6.2 Re-integration support for pupils who have accessed the LSU

Figure 6.2 indicates a possible continuum and differing strategies for supporting pupils who have accessed the Learning Support Unit. The support may include:

• individual support from a key worker on a regular, frequent basis;
• group work with peers to develop strategies;
• less frequent support with a key worker for ongoing monitoring.

This support may be offered by a key person from the LSU or be linked into the school's support systems, including:

• learning mentors
• key teachers offering group work
• Learning Support Department
• SENCO
• Head of Year

depending on the school's pastoral structure.

> **Key points**
>
> ➤ Access to the LSU ideally builds in re-integration from the outset, allowing pupils access to the most positive lessons/ curriculum areas. This limited access reduces the problem of re-integration often experienced after a block of time removed from the main curriculum and peer groups. It also signals to all pupils the main aim of a programme in the LSU, which is to facilitate full re-integration to all their lessons.
> ➤ Parents need to be fully involved in the process.
> ➤ Pupils need to be involved in assessment, target setting and planning for their needs.
> ➤ Units with linked schools need to ensure that all partners are fully involved in the process of planning and implementation of the LSU strategies.
> ➤ While the pupil is accessing the LSU, support can be offered by staff in the unit with time set aside for re-integration issues, developing coping strategies, etc. During this time targets set from the CISS can be discussed and amended and further plans made for more extensive integration.
> ➤ Once the pupils are re-integrating more fully, support in the LSU may consist of just group work support. Alternatively the pupil may be filtered back into other support structures within the school.
> ➤ Ideally group work and target setting will be used as an early intervention strategy and this approach can also be used as part of the support package for pupils who have been in the LSU.
> ➤ An important part of any support package is monitoring pupils' success and the responses of staff to the pupils. The monitoring offers opportunities to deal with a problem before it becomes an issue. LSU staff, learning mentors or another teacher nominated as the key person can do this monitoring. Some of the monitoring can be done in a group work session; this feeds into the approach already mentioned where a group of peers offer help and support to each other in terms of strategies and skills.
> ➤ The LSU needs to be firmly embedded in the school so that all staff are part of the support offered.

Food for thought

There is considerable debate about the use of and usefulness of both Learning Support Units and Pupil Referral Units. This debate often revolves around whether marginalising pupils to a 'unit' in either location is another way of firmly locating the blame within child (Watkins and Wagner 2000). The debate is necessary and important but will not be rehearsed here. The focus of this book is more about helping practitioners make the most out of the provision they can access for pupils and to encourage thinking about wider issues of support around the re-integration of pupils accessing such provision.

Questions

How can you ensure that the LSU you are involved in setting up is not seen as a 'sin bin' where 'unmanageable' pupils are sent?

How can the LSU be firmly embedded in the school's culture in a positive way?

Who needs to be involved in the debate?

What language will you agree to use as a school staff with pupils when describing the LSU?

Chapter 7

Pastoral Support Programmes (PSPs)

Questions this chapter aims to answer

Why do we need Pastoral Support Programmes?

Who might be involved in a Pastoral Support Programme?

What preparation is needed before a Pastoral Support Programme meeting?

What strategies could be used as part of the Pastoral Support Programme process?

What examples of good practice are there?

What makes a successful Pastoral Support Programme?

Early intervention	Learning Support Unit	Pastoral Support Programme	Pupil Referral Unit
Coping in School Scale (CISS) and programme	Referral process Coping in School Scale (CISS)	Systematic assessment Coping in School Scale (CISS)	Re-integration programme Re-integration Readiness Scale (RRS)
	Intervention programme	Target setting	Group work
Code of Practice (COP) Stage 2 (New COP School Action)	Code of Practice (COP) Stage 3 (New COP School Action Plus)	Code of Practice (COP) Stage 3 (New COP School Action Plus)	

Re-integration	Re-integration	Re-integration
SUPPORT		

Figure 7.1 A continuum of support for pupils with emotional and behavioural difficulties

As part of the *Social Inclusion: Pupil Support* guidance, Circulars 10/99 and 11/99 (DfEE 1999a,b), schools are required to put in place strategies to prevent pupils being permanently excluded. This is in response to growing concerns about the long-term social implications of excluding pupils and to research reflecting the key groups of pupils it affects. Young people excluded from school are more likely to:

- be looked after by the local authority
- be involved in offending behaviour (65% of school-age offenders

sentenced in court are non-attenders or have been excluded from school);
- be from specific at-risk groups: male; black; have a statement of special educational needs;
- experience health and housing problems (INCLUDE 2000).

Eighty per cent of pupils excluded from secondary schools and 92 per cent of those excluded from primary schools are boys. Currently only one third of those permanently excluded from school find their way back into mainstream education. Such failure is closely linked to a drastic reduction of life-chances for many young people: unemployment (seven out of ten habitual truants leave school without any exam passes), crime (school non-attenders are up to three times more at risk of being involved in crime – 30 per cent of prisoners were truants), problem drug use, and often homelessness.   (Bentley 1998)

Strategies for keeping young people in school are vital, given the consequences suggested. These requirements encourage schools to look for alternative processes and interventions for pupils who were following particular patterns of behaviour. One such strategy is a Pastoral Support Programme (PSP).

Pupils who do not respond to school actions to combat disaffection may be at serious risk of permanent exclusion or criminal activity, and may need a longer term intervention to keep them from dropping out of school altogether. Teachers should actively identify such young people. Each one will need a Pastoral Support Programme worked up with external services.
                                   (Circular 10/99 (DfEE 1999b))

Obviously the aim is always to intervene and offer support at an earlier stage of the continuum if possible (see Figure 7.1). If a pupil is still finding it hard to cope in school, in spite of all the obvious in-school strategies being used, a PSP is initiated. A PSP is a positive meeting where all those involved with the pupil get together with the pupil (if possible) to put into place a supportive plan of action. Although the reasons why everyone is concerned must be expressed, the meeting is about finding a way forward. Therefore we are not seeking to lay blame but to find alternative strategies for the pupil and school to try.

Pastoral Support Programmes – LEA support

There is great variation in how the PSP process has been put into practice in different schools and LEAs. Some LEAs have taken a whole-authority approach, which has proved particularly effective. One such approach will be discussed in detail to illustrate an example of good practice.

Wandsworth LEA was proactive in implementing the PSP process and issued guidance to schools in October 1999. In this guidance key personnel were identified who could advise and assist schools in implementing good practice in Pastoral Support Programmes. To make this a manageable process and to enable schools to realistically have access to the support and guidance on offer, key personnel were identified by Code of Practice stages. For primary pupils at Stages 1 to 3 of the Code of Practice the primary Behaviour and Learning Support Service was identified as key to the process. This service offers support to schools for pupils already at Stage 3 of the Code of Practice and participating in the PSP process with schools enables the Support Service to build on good practice already established. It was anticipated that there would only be a small number of primary pupils on PSPs and this has been the case in practice. For pupils at Stages 4 and 5 of the Code of Practice the Educational Psychology Service would be the LEA representative at both primary and secondary schools. Obviously sometimes there is overlap where a pupil is referred to the Educational Psychology Service as part of the PSP and then there is a gradual handover process. For all LEA representatives who are involved in PSPs there is the opportunity to liaise and network on a regular basis, which is vital if development of best practice is to be maintained.

The Inclusion Pilot Project and the secondary Pupil Referral Unit both support the PSP process for secondary pupils at Stages 1 to 3 of the Code of the Practice. There were a number of reasons for this decision.

1. It was anticipated that there would be quite a high number of secondary pupils who would need PSPs, based on the fact that there was a higher number of permanent exclusions in the secondary than in the primary phase.
2. The Inclusion Pilot Project was already working in all the secondary schools using the Coping in Schools programme and working closely with the secondary Pupil Referral Unit.
3. If the process was clearly linked with support from the Inclusion team and the PRU, more effective links between institutions could be forged.
4. If pupils needed to be dual registered at the PRU as part of their PSP, contacts and arrangements could be made immediately and the PRU would also have a clear idea of pupils possibly needing dual registration or in danger of being permanently excluded.

The CISS and Pastoral Support Programmes

It was also suggested that as part of the PSP process the Coping in Schools Scale be used as a baseline assessment (for those pupils who had not been assessed at a previous point on the continuum, see Figure 7.1). The idea was that the CISS could be used as a baseline assessment to clarify what was working well and what was problematic across curriculum areas in order that intervention and support could be most effectively targeted. The aim would be to keep pupils in lessons that worked well and target any support groups at lessons that were problematic. This strategy is also discussed in Chapter 6.

It also meant that the systematic assessment of problems was established early on in the PSP process and information was gathered ready for meetings so that all involved could usefully spend time looking at possible strategies.

A main initial focus of the work was around planning and implementation of PSPs. Schools were offered consultation prior to setting up PSP meetings where documentation, intervention strategies already implemented and possible plans for next steps could be discussed. Most schools requested this support. The Coping in Schools Scale is used as part of this process for target setting and planning for effective support.

In Wandsworth LEA's OFSTED inspection in 2000 the implementation of this process was praised:

> Intensive work in both phases is fully in line with the Government's social inclusion strategy and is focusing to good effect on pastoral support programmes and school re-integration plans. A key element of all the work by these services is the development of strategies to help primary and secondary schools develop robust in-school practices that enable them to handle their own difficulties and problems.

Consultation

The format that follows is the sort of advice that has been given to secondary schools who want to set up effective PSPs. In primary schools the process in Wandsworth has been different. All pupils who start the PSP process should have already been identified and worked with by the Behaviour and Learning Support Service and the PSP is therefore a continuation of this work. If no such strategy already exists for your school the approach suggested would work equally well for pupils at primary and secondary levels. Much of this you may already be doing but some of it may be new or different. As with most work with challenging pupils, new ideas are always valuable. There is no final answer but the process set up across one LEA has led to many successful PSPs for pupils and schools.

Guidelines for the first meeting

Preparation

The preparation before a PSP is initiated is very important. Everyone involved needs to be as fully informed as possible in order to develop useful strategies and make pertinent decisions. Prior to the PSP meeting, some form of communication with the parents needs to take place, if possible. Only you will know the level of communication needed to get individual parents on board. Some parents are working and would value a phone call or letter rather than being invited to yet another meeting at school. For other parents a meeting may be advisable so that they feel supported and informed before a meeting where more people will be present. The pupil needs to have time with a supportive adult who can explain the process and perhaps even talk through the possible courses of action that are available for support. It is important that the pupil's views are represented. The pupil should also complete the Coping in Schools Scale (CISS) at this stage (if he or she has not already completed one) with a supportive member of staff and if possible set some targets. The aim is to establish communication between all parties.

Information

In order that the PSP meeting progresses in a spirit of partnership it is important for parents/carers to be fully informed about strategies the school has tried. Those parents/carers who have a good relationship with the school and who are in frequent contact may well be in full possession of all this information. It is sometimes the case that parents/carers are not part of a working relationship with the school, for whatever reason. It is important that a working relationship is re-established if possible. Parents/carers need to feel empowered at the meeting to comment on the targets set and their child's progress over time.

Prior to the PSP meeting it is helpful if certain information is sent to all the people who will be attending the meeting (a list is given in the panel below). In addition, a list of all those attending should be sent to the parents/carers, with explanations of their roles and why they are attending (if this is not sent then these introductions should be made at the beginning of the PSP meeting). Although it takes more planning and organisation to send information out beforehand, this can greatly assist at the meeting as key issues can be addressed immediately.

Information that should be circulated for a PSP meeting

- Copies of the last two or three Individual Education Plans (IEPs) and review reports of those IEPs if these are available.
- Copies of reports about any other intervention strategies used, i.e. Learning Support Unit, learning mentor, other relevant projects.
- Results of the review of the pupil's literacy skills.
- Results of the assessment from subject teachers and tutors using the CISS.
- Results of the pupil's own assessment using the CISS.
- Incident reports.
- Attendance record.

Individual Education Plans

The guidance (DfEE 1999b) states that as part of the PSP process the pupil's Individual Education Plan should be reviewed (therefore suggesting an IEP should be in place). We have certainly advised schools that once a PSP is initiated the pupil needs a Stage 3 IEP as at this stage the school is asking for outside agencies to become involved, if they have not been involved before. One of the interesting links that seem to be being made across some schools is with challenging behaviour and the whole SEN process. In many schools SEN and behaviour had been dealt with quite separately, with the result that pupils with emotional and behavioural difficulties were seen as 'naughty', 'disruptive' and 'challenging' and not regarded as having special needs. It has been a significant shift in thinking in some schools to see pupils with these problems as having special needs. As a consequence, instead of following a discipline route, strategies for support and differentiation are considered. The information from the CISS is being used in some schools to inform IEPs. The process of pupils rating themselves and being involved in the target setting process is good practice for setting IEP targets.

Those people who are involved with the pupil should be invited to the meeting, e.g. social workers, Educational Welfare Officer, Youth Offending Team member, or others, as appropriate for that pupil. The purpose is to have as informed a discussion as possible about all that is happening in that pupil's life. For example, we may not want to suggest additional one-to-one counselling in school if the social worker has just set up something similar. You can also check with parents/carers whether there are other support agencies that they and their families are using and if they would like a representative to attend. Wherever possible the pupils themselves should attend the meeting as the more they are involved the more likely they are to take ownership of the process. For young children, however, you may feel that attending the whole meeting is too much and attending part is more appropriate. Some pupils have a lot of adults involved in their lives and may not want to attend the meeting. It is advisable for a smaller group of supportive adults to meet with the pupil (before the meeting if possible) and afterwards relay the suggestions made in the meeting and invite feedback from the pupil. (This strategy seems to work well where the pupil has been involved in the preparation for the meeting and set his or her own targets.)

There are a number of things that need to be fully explored in this meeting. These may be things that have been looked at in the past and need to be revisited, if only to confirm that this avenue has been explored and is not fruitful for this pupil. A strategy tried previously may be appropriate to try again if we are at a different stage in the pupil's life or learning. The pupil's views need to be sought and considered. Any strategy that the pupil feels positive about has more chance of success. Strategies that could be considered include:

Key points for a PSP meeting

Using existing in-school support:

- harnessing support already in classes the pupil attends;
- peer support or peer mentoring programmes if these are in place;
- assigning the pupil a learning mentor;
- use of the Learning Support Unit if this has not already been used;
- referral to an in-school counsellor (if one is available).

Making changes to existing programmes:

- changing the pupil's tutor group or class;
- changing the pupil's set or group for one or a number of subjects;
- looking at alternative curriculum programmes (for pupils at KS4).

Referral to outside agencies:

- dual registration with the PRU;
- referral to the Educational Psychologist;
- referral to Child and Adolescent Mental Health Services (CAMHS);

- links to other agencies that may offer advice, support, youth programmes;
- involvement of the Educational Welfare Service (EWS).

Summary of what the meeting should cover

- Clear and informative introductions of all the people present so that the parents/carers are clear about the supportive nature of the input.
- Current IEP to be reviewed.
- Clear and reasonable targets to be set, with clarity about how these targets will be monitored.
- A clear plan from the school about intervention strategies to be tried.
- Parents/carers given the opportunity to express their views.
- Clear allocation of tasks to relevant parties.
- Plans for future meetings to review the programme put in place.

An example of the pro-forma used in PSP meetings is shown in Appendix 8.

What will happen after the meeting?

The way the programme is put into place after the meeting is crucial to its success. The pupil needs to have an allocated key person/ supportive adult. This person monitors the pupil's progress on targets on a daily basis and offers advice and support. This supportive adult must be someone with whom the pupil already has a relationship or someone with whom he or she is happy to work. If there are changes to groups to be made, or amendments to the curriculum, these should be completed as soon as possible. Any referrals to be made to outside agencies need to be organised. It is often the case that the key person meets with the pupil either that day or the next to run through what has been discussed and actions to be taken. Even if the pupil was present for the entire meeting such clarification of what was decided is helpful. It provides an opportunity for the pupil to express anxieties or concerns about the strategies discussed.

There needs to be regular review of the PSP by means of all those involved meeting again. This should take place every four to six weeks. At these meetings the targets and strategies that have been put into place need to be evaluated to see if progress is being made. Any changes that need to be made to the suggested strategies can then be decided on.

If a dual registration with the Pupil Referral Unit was suggested as part of the programme, meetings will need to be arranged and visits planned. More details of this process are discussed below.

Summary

- The pupil's targets need to monitored by a key member of staff on a daily basis.
- Actions planned in the meeting need to be implemented.
- A review meeting needs to be held on a regular basis (four to six weeks) with all those involved with the pupil. Progress needs to be reviewed and alternative strategies put in place if progress is not being made.

One strategy suggested as part of a Pastoral Support Programme might be dual registration with the Pupil Referral Unit. Circular 10/99 (DfEE 1999b) suggest this as a possible strategy: 'consider jointly registering the pupil at the school and a Pupil Referral Unit providing the opportunity to benefit from the PRU's expertise while remaining at school, aiding full re-integration later'. (DfEE 1996)

Dual registration needs to be carefully considered to balance the pupil's needs with the difficulties of attending two places of learning. There are a number of important points to make about this strategy. Dual registration should be just that: pupils should attend both institutions and be seen as part of both. Communication between the two institutions is vital so that teachers on both sites are fully appraised of the way the placements are working. Although the PSPs should be reviewed regularly, incidents occur which need to be immediately passed on to the other placement; such incidents are verbal or physical assaults on peers or teachers, situations at home that may affect behaviour, any type of exclusion, sudden changes in attendance patterns. It is advisable to have a weekly contact of some sort during the period of dual registration so that all parties feel fully informed; these could, for example, be a weekly fax of attendance and a behaviour summary.

All dual-registered pupils should also come with baseline data, which as the process becomes embedded will enable the PRU to work more effectively with pupils from the outset.

Dual registration with the Pupil Referral Unit

Where pupils are dual registered at the PRU the ultimate aim is always full re-integration to mainstream school. The break from five days a week in one institution can provide time for reflection, for work on social skills and to catch up on work missed. The time in school needs to be given practical consideration because even two half-day sessions at the PRU will interfere with attendance at lessons at school. For example, the pupil may be missing two out of five English lessons, which makes it difficult to participate in the three lessons he or she is still attending. Where pupils are dual registered these sorts of issues inevitably will arise. They are not insurmountable but careful thought does need to be given to supporting pupils in both environments. It has been found that pupils who are dual registered with schools that are geographically closer to the PRU seem to be the most successful. It is not clear whether this is because half-day sessions are more easily managed or simply due to the logistics of getting to the PRU. If the journey times are shorter between home/school/PRU, it is easier to work out programmes that maximise pupil strengths and lead to the pupil missing fewer lessons. Once the PSP process is under way it is important that communication between the two institutions is well established. The regular reviews of the PSP ensure that the balance of provision is regularly considered and adjustments can be made accordingly.

The PRU's role and client group at the secondary PRU in Wandsworth has changed as a result of successful inclusion and

Re-integration – aim and practice

interventions in secondary mainstream schools. There is less permanent exclusion and so the number in this group has declined and concurrently there are greater numbers of dual-registration pupils. The PRU has had to adapt quickly to the new demands placed upon it and providing appropriate courses for those on PSPs has been a major consideration. One option is to try to develop short intervention programmes that are likely to be relevant, such as drug awareness (in conjunction with local drug prevention provision). The pupils on PSPs have been worked with in separate groups from pupils who are permanently excluded.

Benefits of the PSP process

Experience has demonstrated that there are a number of benefits associated with the proactive approach to the PSP process that has been developed. The first benefit is part of the wider inclusion initiatives that have been enhanced by the PSP process. There is beginning to be a continuum planned for pupils with emotional and behavioural difficulties, particularly in secondary schools where knowledge of and planning for pupils can become more fragmented. Schools are participating in the process with commitment and flexibility and there have been definite developments in the way the process is being used in schools. These developments have included:

Positive attitudes:

(a) Meetings are generally very positive and are conducted in a spirit of partnership between school, parents, pupils and other agencies.
(b) Pupils are increasingly seeing the process as positive and supportive of their needs.

Processes:

(c) Schools are flexibly attempting to use all available resources both in and out of school.
(d) Meetings are becoming increasingly multi-agency and this is enabling greater understanding of the situations involved and also informing possible strategies to be tried.
(e) Schools are very positive about the support that is offered (by LEA representatives).
(f) Dual registrations at the PRU are increasingly being appropriately used.
(g) The increased contact with the PRU and the secondary schools has enabled further development of re-integration arrangements for pupils.

Evaluation:

(h) The need for IEPs to be reviewed as part of the process has led to an emphasis on up-to-date and usable behavioural IEPs.
(i) This emphasis ((h) above) has led to whole-school systems reviews in some schools.

Cross borough:

(j) There has been an increase in representatives from other boroughs attending (where pupils are resident in other boroughs).

In stopping to take a snapshot look at the benefits of the process a few salient features stood out:

- There is a decrease in the number of permanently excluded pupils being referred to the PRU.
- Of the pupils who have been on PSPs less than 10 per cent have been permanently excluded.
- Some schools are planning and setting up quite different and flexible options for pupils at Key Stage 4 who are having difficulties maintaining their places in school.
- The LEA target for exclusions for secondary schools is on track.
- The majority of secondary schools have a decrease in exclusions in line with Government guidelines.

The use of the Coping in Schools Scale as part of the Pastoral Support Programme process has not only informed this process but has led to schools suggesting the importance of early intervention as well as the role of the CISS and programme within this. The information gained from the CISS is also providing prompts in other settings, such as helping learning mentors and tutors in their work with individual pupils. The opportunities for planning and implementing the process and the increased contact with schools have facilitated the work of the Inclusion Project team

Cross-fertilisation – PSPs as part of wider inclusion

It is worth reflecting on what makes a successful Pastoral Support Programme. The following examples of good practice are drawn from successful implementation of the guidance.

Features of a successful PSP

Pupil involvement:

- Pupil fully involved in the process.
- Targets set are pupil-generated.

Family and school:

- Parents actively involved and supportive.
- Open lines of communication between schools and parents are maintained.

Prior to the meeting:

- Views of all teachers of the pupils sought via a baseline assessment of the problems (e.g. CISS).
- There is a clear understanding of school and pupil perspectives through the use of the assessment.
- There is a clear commitment to dealing with difficult behaviours in school, if possible.
- Links with learning mentors for support and guidance are established.

At the meeting:

- Senior management who can take immediate decisions are involved and present at the meeting.
- Year Head or tutor (secondary) or class teacher (primary) are involved and present at the meeting.
- All other professionals involved with the child are present or informed.
- All parties actively seek a solution to the problems.
- The pupil has an allocated key person.
- A support network in school is established for the pupil.
- The LEA representative is actively involved to offer support and guidance.

Maintaining the process:

- The PSP is regularly reviewed (at four- to six-week intervals).
- If dual registration is part of the PSP, communication links are set up and maintained.
- Positive progress is celebrated.
- Solutions are sought to problems presenting themselves.
- Meetings are kept as positive and forward thinking as possible.
- Information on the programme is available to teachers at school, who are encouraged to participate in offering positive support to pupils.

Key points

➤ Pastoral Support Programmes are put in place for pupils at risk of permanent exclusion.
➤ Pastoral Support Programmes need careful planning and monitoring.
➤ Parents and pupils need to be fully involved in the process.
➤ Prior to a meeting, baseline information on the pupil's strengths and weaknesses needs to be gathered.
➤ Outside agencies involved with the pupil and family should be invited to the meeting.
➤ The meeting should be positive and purposeful in drawing up a strategy for supporting the pupil.
➤ The LEA representative should offer support and guidance during the process.
➤ Dual registration with the PRU should be clearly planned and monitored.
➤ Taking a whole LEA approach has many positive benefits.

Food for thought

The educational disadvantage suffered by looked-after children is so extreme that, at present, only the most resilient have any chance of success.
(Jackson 2000)

Given the facts presented at the beginning of this chapter and the quotation above we have a specific need to put in place effective strategies for looked-after children.

Questions

How are looked-after children supported in your school?

Is there a whole-school policy on developing the potential of this group of pupils?

What links do you foster with social services and other involved agencies to ensure that key people in school are aware of these pupils' present situations?

If a pupil who is looked-after needs a PSP how are you going to ensure that this process is supportive and helpful to the pupil?

How might this process tie in with other plans and programmes for the pupil, e.g. Personal Education Plans?

Chapter 8

Re-integration from Pupil Referral Units

Questions this chapter aims to answer

What are the key issues that we need to consider when re-integrating pupils from an off-site unit?

What information do receiving schools need about pupils re-integrating?

What support will pupils and receiving schools need to facilitate the transfer process?

How can a pupil re-integrating access pastoral and support systems to facilitate the transfer?

What are stages of the process?

How might effective school liaison systems be implemented?

What support might be needed post-transfer?

Early intervention	Learning Support Unit	Pastoral Support Programme	Pupil Referral Unit
Coping in School Scale (CISS) and programme	Referral process Coping in School Scale (CISS) Intervention programme	Systematic assessment Coping in School Scale (CISS) Target setting	Re-integration programme Re-integration Readiness Scale (RRS) Group work
Code of Practice (COP) Stage 2 (New COP School Action)	Code of Practice (COP) Stage 3 (New COP School Action Plus)	Code of Practice (COP) Stage 3 (New COP School Action Plus)	

Re-integration	Re-integration	Re-integration
SUPPORT		

Figure 8.1 A continuum of support for pupils with emotional and behavioural difficulties

Chapter 6 considered the role of the Learning Support Unit in providing support within the continuum for pupils with challenging behaviour. A process was outlined that looked at referral procedures, group programmes, re-integration and post-re-integration support. In this chapter the role of the Pupil Referral Unit (PRU) in the continuum of support will be considered. A process will be outlined that considers the identification of pupils who are ready to re-integrate, group programmes, pre-transfer visits and post-transfer support. Pupil Referral Units vary in the provision they offer and the range of pupils they work with. All, however, are involved in trying to either re-integrate pupils to mainstream school, college placements or the world of work. The main focus of this programme would be re-integration to mainstream school but the same process would be beneficial in preparing pupils for college or work.

Pupils may attend the PRU for varying amounts of time. Some pupils are dual registered with the PRU and a mainstream school and may attend both provisions during the week (dual registration is also discussed in Chapter 7). Some pupils have been permanently excluded and the PRU will be providing all of their education. There are also other groups of pupils who may attend a PRU, such as teenage mothers, school refusers, and pupils who have no school place for other reasons.

The key differences between PRUs and schools include:

- a management committee instead of a governing body;
- dual registration of pupils in PRUs and schools;
- staffing and relative duties of LEAs and teachers in charge;
- the curriculum, which need not be the full National Curriculum.
(Circular 11/99 (DfEE 1999c))

PRUs are off-site units and the pupils, whether dual registered or with no school place, are attending not only a different building but also generally a 'school' that runs in a different way from the mainstream from which they came or are attending for the rest of the week. It is very different from a Learning Support Unit discussed in Chapter 6. You may, however, discern many overlapping features in terms of information, support and systems that need to be considered to ensure a successful re-integration. In some schools the LSU may play an integral role in re-integrating pupils from the PRU; in others this role may be strategically avoided. Either system can work effectively if the key issues are considered and solutions to potential problems devised.

Individual Re-integration Plans

Each excluded pupil should have an Individual Re-integration Plan (IRP) as detailed in DfEE Circular 11/99. This plan should include:

- steps to be taken for re-integration into school;
- dates for the LEA officer to review the re-integration plan (at least monthly);
- the name of the school to which the child will return;
- a programme of re-integration with the named school;
- the target date for return to school.

In practice, IRPs including this level of detail, especially the name of school and return date, can be difficult to maintain for all pupils. Some pupils, for example, may be undergoing statutory assessment while they are attending the PRU and it is not possible or appropriate to name a school until this process has been completed. However, the guidance (DfEE Circular 11/99) clearly indicates the need for re-integration to be the primary strategy for pupils excluded and offers a framework within which such a plan should be conducted. The programme outlined in this chapter would assist PRUs in meeting the requirements of the IRP.

Re-integrating pupils from an off-site unit – issues

Many primary PRUs have great success re-integrating pupils and few issues arise about finding schools willing to re-integrate a pupil. This is often not the case with secondary PRUs, which may have very few secondary schools to work with in the LEA and a larger number of permanently excluded pupils. The following suggestions could apply equally well in both phases.

Information, support and systems

As discussed in Chapter 6 about Learning Support Units, the sort of information shared, the support put in place, how this fits into the existing system, and how this system might need to change, are all vital issues to consider when we are planning for a successful re-integration.

Information

It is important to consider the information needed by the receiving school. There are various sorts of information that might be useful for planning purposes. This might be information concerning:

- *The amount of time the pupil has been out of school.*
  This will be important as receiving teachers need to understand the sorts of fears or apprehensions that the pupil may have. It will also be important for planning the type of induction the pupil might require; for example, if a pupil has only been out of school for a term they will still be familiar with the routines and demands of a mainstream environment. However, if they have been out of school for two years, or never attended a secondary school, it may take quite some time for routines to become familiar and manageable.
- *The reasons why a pupil was attending the PRU.*
  A pupil who has been permanently excluded will need different levels and types of support than pupils who have been attending the PRU because they were too frightened to attend school or pupils for whom no school placement was available.
- *The sort of programme that the pupil has accessed at the PRU.*
  This information will help in planning which subject areas a pupil might need support with and those that have been sufficiently covered. It will also be important to know the amount of time the pupil has been on a full-time programme or if a full-time programme has not been possible for some reason.
- *The type and amount of re-integration preparation the pupil has received.*
  If pupils have been part of a re-integration group for a term and have had several school visits they may need different post-

transfer support from pupils being re-integrated within one month of leaving their last school.

- *Baseline data on academic skills as well as information on readiness to re-integrate, including strengths and weaknesses on behavioural criteria.*
  It is important that the receiving school is aware of the pupil's possible areas of conflict or distress so that support and understanding can be developed accordingly. It is equally important to emphasise a pupil's strengths so that these can be developed and enhanced to promote the pupil's self-esteem and sense of achievement.

- *Ways to work with parents/pupils that have been successful in the past.*
  If there are successful strategies that have been developed for working with the pupil and the pupil's parents/carers these should be shared. If the pupil receives little support at home or is likely to be affected by home circumstances, this information enables mainstream staff to respond with support and understanding. Equally, if parents are supportive and have worked in partnership with the PRU, the receiving school can build upon this.

Support

Support for pupils re-integrating is vital. In the first instance this needs to be hands-on support in the school. This support is important not only for the pupil but also for the school – both need to feel supported in the process of transition.

There are two areas of support that need careful planning and clarity. One is support for the pupil and one is support for the receiving school. Although the two areas of support are working towards the same end-goal, the successful re-integration of the pupil, they might involve different support activities. Chapter 2 provides a summary of key aspects of successful support and the following sections build on those aspects.

Support for pupils

Supporting the pupil through the transition stages is vital. Individuals all need different levels of support and there is not a blueprint for necessary contact time. What is needed is a system for supporting pupils that will make the school feel empowered to employ a positive approach and can be utilised according to individual needs. Prior to the transfer pupils will need to consider and discuss the sort of problems they might face on transfer. Being aware that problems exist helps those supporting to prepare responses and survival strategies. Pupils also need to spend time talking about the things they are looking forward to, whether this is joining up with friends or access to good sports facilities. School visits, once a school is allocated, help to put worries in context, although this does not always mean the worries are reduced. For pupils who are concerned about the number of other pupils and the size of the building a visit may confirm these fears and this in turn will be important information in terms of any future planning for that pupil's re-integration. The process outlined in the rest of this chapter offers practical strategies for implementing support for pupils.

Support for the receiving school

The receiving school needs support in a number of ways. Helpful information, well disseminated, is needed, as discussed above. It helps communication between the PRU and the school during the initial stages of transfer if there is a key contact person in each institution who knows the pupil and the situations likely to occur. Receiving schools generally value any advice that supporting PRU staff can give about the management of the pupil's behaviour. Many PRUs offer outreach support to mainstream schools and may offer training and advice about behaviour management generally. This advice and support would be well timed to coincide with a re-integration. The school as well as the pupil will need to be clear about the level, timing and duration of post-transfer support. Support in school on a regular basis is a key ingredient of successful re-integration, helps receiving schools feel supported and builds long-term partnerships between the PRU and schools that aid subsequent re-integrations. The development of networks with schools is time-consuming but essential. The process outlined in the rest of this chapter includes practical strategies for implementing support for schools.

Systems

PRU staff may need to have information about the receiving school's systems to facilitate the re-integration process for both pupil and school. Consideration needs to be given to the school's pastoral and support systems and how a pupil re-integrating can access these. The allocation to the pupil of a key supportive person from within the school is helpful in identifying to whom to go if a concern arises. Pupils re-integrating will also need to be clear about the school's discipline structures and systems of reward. They will need to have clear guidance about timings of the day, lunch-time procedures, assembly protocol, after-school activities, etc. The key supportive person may need to remind pupils of these systems and procedures many times.

Consideration needs to be given to changes in or enhancements to the support systems in a school, especially those arising because problems present a challenge to the existing system. Outreach support from the PRU may be appropriate. The support from the PRU might be able to forge links between existing networks to promote more inclusive practice, for example creating stronger links between learning mentors, Heads of Year and the Learning Support Unit.

Stages of the process

Assessment and target setting
Re-integration group
School liaison (staff)
School visits (pupils)
Re-integration
Post-transfer support

Assessment and target setting

A first stage of the re-integration programme is to assess the pupils with the Re-integration Readiness Scale (RRS) (McSherry 1996). Initially staff in the PRU would complete this process. As many staff as possible would complete the RRS to get the fullest profile of the pupil's behaviour and coping skills at that point. Some PRUs are using the RRS as a more systematic ongoing assessment of a pupil's behavioural progress, in which case it would be deciding at which point the pupil is ready to join a re-integration group. Once pupils have been identified for re-integration preparation they complete the RRS themselves and set a target based on their rating of themselves. The completion of the assessment tool and target setting process is explained in more detail in Chapter 5 and it would be advisable to re-read this section now so as to familiarise yourself with the suggested process and outcomes.

Parents/carers need to be part of the process from the outset. How this involvement is coordinated and maintained will depend to some extent on the relationship already established with the parents/carers. A meeting with all involved is often useful but some parents may find this difficult. It is important that parents are positive and supportive of the process.

Figure 8.2 shows a process flowchart for re-integration of pupils from the PRU.

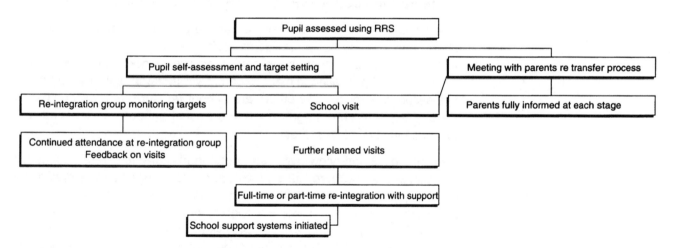

Figure 8.2 Re-integration process flowchart

Re-integration group

It is important to stress that being part of the re-integration group is only part of the re-integration programme that the pupil will receive at the PRU. Once a pupil is preparing to return to mainstream, all the work completed at the PRU will be focused on this aim. All staff at the PRU will be involved in helping pupils achieve their targets.

The assessment tool is the first part of a process that now continues in the group. Ideally the group is fairly static because in order for pupils to develop supportive relationships with peers and feel confident in the group work process the group cannot be subject to continual change. However, there will be certain ebb and flow as pupils are re-integrated and some pupils will need a longer preparation period than others. It is certainly important that the same adult or adults facilitate this group each week. If your staffing allows for it then running groups with two supportive adults can be very helpful. Pupils are able to see adults working cooperatively and this is a also useful way to introduce new staff or existing staff who wish to take on a new role in the process.

A good starting place for this group is for pupils to reflect on what they did and did not like about their last school. It is important for pupils to be allowed to express these feelings and share them with others. They will probably find that other peers share similar feelings and experiences as well as different situations. It may also be worth sharing at this initial stage hopes and fears for re-integration. Re-integration needs to be revisited on a regular basis, as pupils' concerns will change over time. With some groups you can move straight into active discussion and they will participate. With other groups this may take longer and it is advisable to have some games or exercises to use with the group as the pupils get to know each other. Group work resources are listed at the end of Chapter 5. Pupils review their targets on a weekly basis using the Pupil Action Plan (see Figure 2.2).

Case Study 8.1

The use of the Re-integration Readiness Scale and Re-integration Groupwork at Francis Barber Pupil Referral Unit

Pupils who are at Francis Barber are outside of mainstream education and all are thus in some sense excluded. Referrals are made for a number of reasons: some pupils have been permanently excluded from their original schools, some have failed to make secondary transfer and are not on the roll of a secondary school and others are school refusers. A large number of these pupils have had negative experiences of school and learning and consequently have low self-esteem.

After an initial interview with the pupil and parents/carers, academic assessments are carried out and an appropriate curriculum is drawn up. Some pupils are put onto PSPs before permanent exclusion so there may be additional information already available, including a completed Coping in Schools Scale. These pupils are already likely to be familiar with a scale that is similar to the RRS. Such information can provide a valuable point of reference for the receiving staff at the PRU.

The majority of pupils at Key Stage 3 complete the Re-integration Readiness Scale (RRS) at some stage, even if they are initially deemed unsuitable for inclusion in a re-integration group. For a worthwhile teacher assessment to take place a fair amount of experience of the pupil is needed and therefore the teacher assessment will not take place immediately.

Many pupils find that some of the language and concepts used in the RRS are challenging or unfamiliar. The advantage that this gives is that the self-assessment needs to be completed with the help of a member of staff and means that this is by necessity a discursive and reflective process.

Self-assessment, in conjunction with input from a member of staff, provides an opportunity to examine some behaviours and discuss whether they are in fact appropriate. The assessment can therefore be highly effective in highlighting areas that need development and as a result facilitates target setting. Sometimes initial targets may simply take the form of identification, by the pupils themselves, of when particular behaviours are exhibited. Subsequently work can be done to address the question of what action can be taken to avoid such behaviours.

An essential starting point of re-integration is the students' own acknowledgement and awareness of where their particular challenges lie. A major strength of the RRS lies in the fact that the self-assessment process gives staff a clear indication of the pupils' perceptions of themselves and their current situations. It also provides a good starting point for the pupils to identify areas for development and set worthwhile targets.

Once the assessments are completed the initial focus is on setting targets identified from the RRS. It is valuable to spend a short time discussing what constitutes an effective target. When appropriate targets have been agreed the pupils write them down and initial them to acknowledge that they will try to achieve them. In some cases the first session with an entirely new re-integration group has been used to complete the RRS as a group. This involves the teacher reading through each question, explaining any difficult language, and where appropriate giving examples. After discussion each pupil then rates himself or herself. Clearly the ability to complete the scale as a group in the early stage of its formation will depend on the group dynamics. It may not be an appropriate or successful way to start with some of the more disaffected or reticent pupils.

Subsequent sessions generally start with a group review of the success or otherwise of individual targets. Once the pupils in a group become more confident and at ease with each other they are often prepared to suggest and discuss strategies to help others meet their targets. On occasions, when a target is not being successfully met, there may well be consensus from the group that a target needs to be modified in order for it to be effective.

In that all members of the group have the same eventual aim, i.e. re-integration to school, pupils are generally supportive of their peers and are willing to suggest strategies to help others. For those about to return to school it is also worth considering some worthwhile targets for them to take with them into their new school. Other useful areas for discussion are past experiences of school, particular worries about returning to an unfamiliar school, e.g. where to go if one feels unwell, how to deal with anxieties about particular lessons or situations, and occurrences that are likely to cause confrontation. If one of the pupils has been on a school visit or interview, it can be especially valuable if his or her experiences and impressions are shared with others.

The aims of the re-integration group are to enable pupils to:

• Set appropriate and achievable targets, both for their current setting and when they do return to school.
• Reflect on their own and their peers' progress.
• Discuss any particular anxieties they may have.
• Share the experiences of visits to schools and interviews.
• Share the challenges of re-integration and provide support for each other.

If pupils are initially unaware of the effects of their behaviour on others, or unable to reflect on this behaviour, it is important that you try to address this within the group. It pupils cannot progress on behavioural targets in the PRU it is unlikely to be easier when they return to mainstream school. Pupils need to be making progress on targets before they start to re-integrate. The case study below concerns a student who initially was unable to accept responsibility for his targets. Pupils accepting responsibility for their own behaviour is an integral part of emotional development. While it is important to also discuss the role school systems and even individual teachers might play in making school life more difficult, it is important that pupils are able to develop strategies to deal with these difficult situations.

Case Study 8.2

Peer group support

Background

The PRU had been developing the use of the RRS for identification of pupils. This was the first re-integration group that had been established. The group was a mixture of pupils who had been permanently excluded and pupils who were school 'refusers'. Pupil A had been permanently excluded from his previous secondary school.

Approach

The approach involved five stages.

1. Planning with PRU staff

From April, planning sessions took place with the PRU staff to formulate an integrated approach using the assessment tool to set targets with pupils and to develop a re-integration group. The aims of this group were to:

- set and monitor targets;
- discuss strategies for meeting targets with staff and peers;
- build up a group identity and focus for support and help with problem behaviours;
- discuss problems and worries about re-integration in a focused and supportive atmosphere;
- develop coping strategies for recurring situations.

2. Assessment and target setting

Pupil A joined the re-integration group having completed the RRS himself (staff from the PRU had also completed the RRS on Pupil A). There was a slight mismatch in the ratings between the two, with Pupil A rating himself with 98% and the staff rating him at around 79%.

Pupil A found it difficult at first to indicate anything with which he might have a problem. He felt that any problems he had had were to do with the previous school and not his own behaviour. Any problems he was experiencing at the PRU he felt were not an issue, as he would behave differently once he was in a new school. (This is a not uncommon response with pupils in this situation but it is important to get beyond this attitude and for them to see that developing coping strategies can be useful and transferable.)

After looking at the criteria within the RRS he identified 'arriving quietly for lesson' as something he could work on.

3. Re-integration group

Within the first few sessions Pupil A was quite disruptive at a low level throughout the sessions. He caused distractions for others and was unable to sit quietly and listen. He also interrupted or offered comments at inappropriate times and seemed unaware of this. He tended to overrate his ability to meet his targets and to blame any lapses on reactions to others, which were quite justifiable in his eyes.

Other members of the group, although getting irritated, were generally supportive and tried to ignore his comments. However, after a few weeks they queried his ratings of himself on his targets and some offered helpful suggestions as to how he might avoid confrontation and tone down his reactions. The staff running the group also discussed with him the fact that his interruptions were not always appropriate and why they felt this was the case.

Pupil A initially responded in a mixed way to the suggestions made but over a number of weeks put some of the ideas into practice and found many of them worked well.

4. Outcomes

As Pupil A's behaviour settled down he was more responsive to suggested strategies made by others in the group. His peers also commented positively on his successes. He set himself new targets: 'to arrive at lessons calmly and settle quickly' and 'to be polite to staff and peers, in particular by not interrupting people'.

Pupil A made progress on all his targets and was becoming a valuable and contributing member of the group. At this point a placement was found for him in a secondary school (one of the schools into which the PRU had not previously re-integrated pupils). Pupil A was very positive about this move and made successful preliminary visits and a successful interview. He fed back to the group after each session in his new school and was very positive about his full-time re-integration.

5. Continued support

Pupil A received support for his interview and all his visits to the new school. PRU staff were involved in planning and networking with the mainstream school for the transfer. The PRU also offered support in terms of visits and contact with the transfer school after the pupil had re-integrated.

For Pupil A in the Case Study 8.2, the support and suggestions of his peers in the group played a valuable part of his pre-transfer preparation.

For more detailed suggestions on setting up and running group work you can refer to Chapter 4, where each stage of the process is explained in detail.

School liaison – staff

Links and communications with mainstream schools are a core part of successful re-integration work. If a school can easily access advice or just talk to a designated member of staff at the PRU they are more willing to participate in a partnership process. Although there are similarities with the links discussed in Chapter 6 on Learning Support Units, the links developed with the PRU need to be more formal and systematic because the PRU is an off-site unit and not part of the school.

Key people

It is helpful to have key people in each institution to develop links and establish networks. In the PRU there may be one or two staff who are more actively involved in re-integration or outreach or it may be that staff have designated schools with which they work. With either model it is useful to have one person who coordinates the re-integration process for the PRU and keeps an overview of the process. Within each mainstream school a key person needs to be identified. Positive working relationships between professionals liaising on re-integration is important. Communication needs to be planned and effective.

Network arrangements

Although communication will mainly be through the key person in each institution it is also important to familiarise and perhaps introduce the key person and other professionals who will form a network around the pupil. The network may include the tutor, learning mentor, Educational Welfare Officer, SENCO and others who are relevant to the pupil. It will be helpful to make a note of all involved in the network so that others have details of the main players should they need to deputise for the key person.

Visiting schools

Much of the networking noted above can be most effectively carried out through meeting people face to face on a school visit. The meetings can be arranged formally as you establish your links and then more informally on subsequent school visits. Linking with Heads of Year and tutors through the key person is important before the pupil starts to attend any part of the school day. It is important to establish the school systems that a pupil will need to know; these do vary greatly from one school to another, especially at secondary school.

PRU visits

It will be helpful if school staff can visit the PRU and see the pupil in his or her working environment there. Also, in the initial stages of setting up a link with a mainstream school, it is helpful for staff to see the PRU environment and be aware of how the PRU is run and the sort of curriculum options the pupil may be attending.

Aiding communication with parents

Staff from the PRU can help set up communication links between parents and the school. Advice can be offered on the most effective ways of communicating with individual parents/carers. PRU staff often work very hard to develop trusting relationships with parents and can be helpful and supportive to parents in developing new working relationships with the receiving school.

School visits – pupils

Schools visits are an important part of preparation. Primary pupils will need to meet their new class teacher and their new class. It is often useful if they can experience the playground environment and perhaps work with a small group of pupils who may 'look out' for the new pupil in the first few weeks. These arrangements can be very informal or you could use a more structured approach.

Some secondary pupils re-integrating will not have attended a secondary school. There is a need for them to experience and then reflect upon the size of the school, the number of pupils they will have contact with, lunch-time procedures, lesson changeovers, morning registration routines, etc. Discussions after school visits may elicit new concerns or problems that need to be addressed; for example, the pupil may feel very worried about arriving with so many pupils in the morning. One strategy that could be used in this instance is for the pupil to be met by some pupils who the school identifies as being sensible and supportive. It would be ideal if these pupils are in the same tutor group as the pupil re-integrating. This sort of strategy is often not difficult to set up but does take time. Pupils would need to be identified, and they need to meet with the re-integrating pupil, preferably a few times so that each feels comfortable with the process.

Case Study 8.3 illustrates the use of re-integration group sessions in the proposed mainstream school to assist pupils in preparing for their transfer.

Case Study 8.3

Re-integration group in the mainstream school

Background

A group of five pupils were all working in a re-integration group and all planning to return to the same secondary school. The group had a variety of needs and came from different year groups but several of the pupils had never successfully transferred to a mainstream school. It was felt that a once-a-week re-integration group for the pupils at the proposed school, run by Inclusion Project staff, on behalf of the PRU and linking with key mainstream staff, would be a useful preparation.

Liaison with key staff

Initially the idea was put to the key link teacher in the school. She was very enthusiastic about the additional support for the pupils and the school in respect of the transfer. Two of the pupils were felt to be more in need of additional help and would need to feel very confident in the mainstream environment before a full re-integration could take place. In the first instance only one pupil was going to be attending the school full time. The others attended the re-integration group only. The plan was for others to follow suit (start re-integrating) as this became appropriate. For the pupil re-integrating, links were made with the Head of Year and tutor.

Setting up the group

The group ran for an hour each week on the same day. The session started after the official start to the afternoon, which meant pupils attending did not have to arrive just as the whole school was on the move. The school allocated the same room to be available each week. The group met in this room but if pupils arrived early for the group they had a designated place to go (the Learning Support Department) where they were always made welcome. The group work followed the same pattern as that that had been offered at the PRU:

- monitoring and setting of targets;
- peer support;
- feedback on re-integration experiences as appropriate.

In addition, for those re-integrating, any problems that had arisen could be discussed and dealt with as applicable.

Progress of the group

Within a few weeks the second pupil was ready to begin re-integration. He began on a part-time basis initially, building over four weeks to a full-time placement. Both pupils now re-integrated initially still attended the group as an additional support. For other members of the group the transition was slower.

Benefits of the process

The pupils and the school reported feeling supported by this approach. Communication with staff in the school was made much easier; for example, when the second pupil started his re-integration, meetings with tutor and Year Head could be set up on the same afternoon and a supportive adult was available to be part of that meeting. If there were issues to be sorted out that had arisen during the week these could also be dealt with immediately. For two of the pupils the once-a-week visit enabled them to decide whether they felt they could re-integrate into such a big school. For the third pupil to attempt re-integration it became clear that he would need additional outside support (psychiatrist) to assist in this process.

Outcomes

Of the five who started the process, two have successfully re-integrated full time into the school. A third started the re-integration and is still dual registered but receiving additional external support. Two of the pupils did not go further and attempt re-integration. One of these is now undergoing statutory assessment. An additional pupil who joined the group has now also re-integrated full time in the school with the additional help provided by a statement of special educational need.

Re-integration

Full-time re-integration
In many respects full-time re-integration is preferable:

- The pupil time is not split between two places and they feel they belong in the new school.
- The receiving school takes full responsibility, with support from the PRU, for the pupil. This may still mean that the pupil is dual registered with both institutions in the first instance but all school time is spent in the receiving school.
- The parents are clear about lines of communication because the pupil is now attending the new school.
- There are no issues about lessons in a subject area being attended half of the week and not the other half.
- The pupil gets acclimatised to the new situation more quickly.
- There is less feeling of being on trial at the new school.

Dual registration – both institutions attended for part of the week
This approach to re-integration is more problematic for the opposite of all the reasons stated above. It is important that the part-time re-integration does not last too long because it is difficult to sustain two placements effectively and the pupil may feel a sense of not belonging anywhere. It is also problematic over any length of time from a curriculum viewpoint because it is difficult to coordinate progress if you miss half the input. However, for some pupils this is the right way to re-integrate. It may be that they have a fear of attending school and a gradual re-integration is useful. Additional support can be offered during the process from their session at the PRU.

Post-transfer support

Support for the pupil and the receiving school from the PRU needs to be clearly defined so that everyone knows when it will take place, for how long and how additional advice is accessed if necessary. There are different amounts of support offered from the PRU to schools. Some on-site support on a regular basis in the initial stages is very important. It enables those involved to be in communication and any problems that arise are quickly dealt with.

Case Study 8.4 illustrates an example of a re-integration greatly helped by regular on-site support.

Case Study 8.4

Value of regular support

Pupil B had been to secondary school in Year 7 and not regularly attended since. He was being re-integrated back into Year 10. Obviously with such prolonged absence from school the process was not going to be easy for him. There had also been considerable upheaval within his family during this time, with the prolonged illness of a family member.

Pupil B had attended the PRU and expressed an interest in re-integrating. He joined a group of pupils re-integrating to one secondary school and initially attended a group session run at the mainstream school once a week at the end of Year 9.

At the start of term he was to re-integrate full time to the mainstream secondary school. His attendance at the group once a week was to continue to offer support. On the first day at school there was a re-integration group meeting and when he came to this he reported that he had only attended the first two lessons and then gone home. He had found the sheer numbers of people overwhelming, and added to this there had been timetable and room confusions (as is so often the case in a new school year) which had caused him further confusion and distress. However, he had returned in the afternoon for his group session, which was a very positive sign.

He discussed in the group quite openly how he had found the morning. The others were sympathetic, as for some of them this was a familiar scenario. There were several issues that needed to be sorted out:

1. He had left the school site without informing anyone and this needed to be negotiated.
2. The timetable and room allocation need to be clarified to avoid a repeat of the confusion.
3. He obviously needed a key person within the school to go to if things were not working (an idea he had resisted before re-integration began).
4. Home and school would need close contact over any leaving of the school site.
5. There needed to be greater communication within the school about his possible needs.

In some respects many of these things were better dealt with after his arrival but if he and the school had not been receiving on-site support things might have gone on for several weeks before everyone became aware of the potential damage to the re-integration process. As it was, one of the project team liaised with the Head of Year immediately and negotiated a process for leaving the site. A specific time was allocated for him to go to the Head of Year and sort out the timetable. He was able to talk through his fears with someone immediately and feel the support of his peers within the group.

When he was unable to come in the next morning his mother came to school and saw the Head of Year. She had been fully informed by project staff of the previous day's events and was able to arrange an immediate meeting with the tutor and support staff and a network was quickly established. A note was sent out to all subject teachers to assist them in offering the best opportunities for this pupil within his classes and the school felt empowered, in control and supported at the same time.

Key points

> ➤ Information given to the receiving school should be useful and clear.
> ➤ Subsequent sharing of information between school and PRU is important for positive planning.
> ➤ Support for the pupil during the process of preparation and transfer is essential.
> ➤ Support for the receiving school is important for developing relationships.
> ➤ School systems need to be understood by all involved in the re-integration. Adaptations to the system may be appropriate.
> ➤ Parents need to be involved from the outset.
> ➤ Pupils benefit from assessing their strengths and weaknesses and target setting.
> ➤ Pupils benefit from the support of their peers through the use of re-integration (preparation) groups.
> ➤ Key staff in each institution need to liaise closely throughout the process.
> ➤ Pupils need to visit their new school and meet key people on several occasions if possible.
> ➤ Post-transfer support is a vital part of the process.

Food for thought

Integration versus inclusion debate

This is an interesting debate (Booth 2000) and it will not be rehearsed again but a few additional points will be raised. Simplifying the argument: assimilationist views (the pupil must fit into the system to be included) are associated with the language of integration (whether fairly or not) and transformative views (the system adapts to include the pupil) are associated with inclusion. Use of language is obviously important and the use of language in terms of special needs, as already highlighted in Chapter 1, is influential. A further distinction can be made between integration and re-integration. Re-integration as a process is harder because the pupil has tried and failed within the system once already and therefore the re-integration is fraught with prejudices on both sides and expectations of failure are high. The debate and in fact the reality have moved on in some ways, especially in terms of integration. Pupils are now often in reality more 'included' in the sense that schools are more flexible and open to change in order to enhance the learning of pupils deemed to have special educational needs. However, this is rarely the case for pupils from PRUs and EBD schools who re-integrate. Here a predominantly assimilationist view still exists, with pupils often offered a trial period to see how it works.

In some ways the term 'inclusion' has superseded the term 'integration'. However, the term 're-integration' (of pupils from a PRU or and EBD special school) is still used. Re-integration as a process also still involves pupils fitting into existing structures and it is still rare for much change in the school to be contemplated to accommodate them. Systems cannot be expected to change before giving young people a chance to be included but if the systems can be encouraged to change simultaneously, and be enhanced by the young people being re-integrated, then very positive effects for all will be experienced.

Case Study 8.5

Pupil C

Pupil C had been permanently excluded from a secondary school and spent a term at the PRU. He was doing well at the PRU and was at the end of Year 9. The staff at the PRU felt it would be the best thing if Pupil C tried a re-integration from the beginning of Year 10, with some preparation visits at the end of Year 9.

The secondary school approached for the re-integration was a very inclusive school and had a good relationship with staff from the PRU and behavioural support staff. They agreed to take a group of five pupils, including Pupil C. It was therefore planned to put in place a re-integration programme, including a weekly re-integration group at the school for the pupils but run by LEA Inclusion Project staff.

As is often the case for pupils who have already been permanently excluded, the receiving school was apprehensive as to how Pupil C's re-integration would go. In addition Pupil C's parents were less than supportive, refusing to buy a school uniform because he might not succeed. However, at the end of the summer term in Year 9 Pupil C attended the new school for two days a week for two weeks while also attending the re-integration preparation group on the school site run by project staff.

Within the first week two incidents occurred (both initiated by less than tuned-in staff) that Pupil C dealt with admirably. The school staff who were supporting and monitoring progress (the Year Head and SENCO) were very impressed with Pupil C's handling of the situations and they had actively supported him in sorting them out.

Consequently they were happy to offer a full-time place on dual registration for the autumn term.

Supported initiatives like the project staff running the group, and therefore being in school every week to monitor progress and work with pupils and staff, can offer practical input and support as well as giving schools confidence to try new initiatives and re-integrate larger numbers of pupils.

In the long run it is not about making the learner fit the system and as schools become treated as consumer-led market places the system needs to fit the learner. It is about a system that is flexible enough to accommodate all learners and their varying needs at progressive stages of their learning. It is about learners being able to actively participate in their education at their own level.

Questions

Are views in your school generally assimilationist or transformative?

In what ways might re-integration for pupils from the PRU be made easier? Think of one positive step that could be taken.

How might this process be started in your school?

Chapter 9

Key points of implementation and ways forward

The Coping in Schools programme has three elements:

- Assessment
- Intervention (group work)
- Support

Each of these elements has been discussed in detail in previous chapters.

The programme *challenges beliefs* using a cognitive approach. Pupils and their teachers, by being encouraged to take a complex transactional model approach, reflect on how interactions between them influence their behaviour on subsequent meetings. It has also worked in practice to 'turn around' the school experience of pupils the school felt had no chance of succeeding.

The programme *provides a consistent positive adult relationship* as part of the individual or group work. This process allows pupils a mediator or advocate who is also part of the school system and therefore understands how the pupil's present behaviour is affecting others in the school.

There are *opportunities each week for positive reinforcement* as any success is celebrated, however small. Even in a bad week the pupil will have some positive input.

The CISS aims to assist in *making the task manageable* for the pupil and the supportive adult. Using items that describe specific behaviours helps pupils to set targets.

Identifying a target helps to give a *focus to the process of cognitive change*. It enables pupils and their teachers to concentrate on the focus behaviour and be positive about success in this area.

Success is celebrated always, however small it is.

The Coping in Schools programme challenges beliefs and provides for manageable focused success

The information gained using the CISS presented in this book to assess behaviour can be used in a number of ways:

- The assessment can be used at an early intervention stage, as part of the referral criteria for Learning Support Units, as part of the Pastoral Support Programme process.

Summary of applications of CISS

- To compare teachers' and pupils' perceptions of the problem. In some ways an important starting point for intervention work is being aware of what these differences in perception are and what they might mean.
- To look at a pupil's baseline scores and assess them again after the intervention and analyse the progress made.
- It can also be used in its original application for assessing readiness to re-integrate for pupils in off-site units.
- To gauge measurable difference on a set of criteria. This is important not only for planning with that individual pupil but also for reporting purposes both at school and LEA level.

Summary of applications of group work

Group work can be used:

- At an early intervention stage, for example for primary/secondary transfer as illustrated in Chapter 5, and for pupils whose behaviour is starting to cause concern. This early intervention group work may be facilitated by a learning mentor or class tutor.
- As part of the programme in the Learning Support Unit.
- As part of a planned programme for pupils on Pastoral Support Programmes.
- For pupils planning to re-integrate to mainstream school from the PRU.
- For pupils who have been non-attenders as part of a planned re-integration programme.

There are probably already further applications of the group work that you can think of in your own institution.

Support for pupils

Support for pupils who have accessed intervention at any stage of the continuum is vital and this needs to be planned as a whole-school approach to supporting pupils with emotional and behavioural difficulties and/or challenging behaviours.

Further applications of the Coping in Schools programme

Group targets

As different schools, off-site units and LEAs apply the programme, further possible applications are suggested and tried. For example, the CISS can be completed for a particular class and data analysed to highlight group strengths and weaknesses. Targets can then be set for teachers as well as pupils in relation to improvements in key areas for the whole group. In this context the CISS is being used as a baseline for measuring progress of larger groups of pupils.

The interpersonal and social skills curriculum

The CISS can provide not only a baseline for group strengths and weaknesses but also a social skills curriculum. Work based around developing the competencies within the CISS would offer clear guidelines and structure to an interpersonal and social skills curriculum. This curriculum is in the process of being developed.

Issues to consider

The dynamics of the government's Social Inclusion agenda in schools will inevitably have an effect on schools and on support services and PRUs. It would seem reasonable to suppose that if schools are including young people they may previously have been excluding, they might be more reluctant to re-integrate others. It may also alter the clientele of the PRU, with those pupils eventually being permanently excluded being much harder to work with and re-integrate (in terms of the excluded part of a PRU's client group).

Pastoral Support Programmes seem to be achieving very positive results and schools are being creative and positive about working with pupils who are experiencing difficulties. The use of a systematic assessment tool and Wandsworth's proactive approach to schools through giving LEA support in implementing this process seems to have been well received by schools across the authority. Permanent exclusion figures as well as the number of successful PSPs would seem to indicate that it has been very effective in enabling both schools and the LEA to meet targets set.

In creating an integrated LEA approach, movement across institutions has become more meaningful. PRU and school can start working with a pupil using information from a programme that all institutions are implementing. It has helped to make the PSP process a proactive one, with schools increasingly able to access and utilise the range of possibilities both within schools and jointly with outside provision for pupils who are finding school a challenge.

A final word about relationships

The key to successfully working with pupils with challenging behaviours is the development of supportive relationships. Teachers and pupils need to develop strategies for effectively working together. The approach explained and the applications of it keep teachers and pupils central to the process of change. However well systems are set up and monitored, the vital component for success is the relationship between teachers and their pupils.

Food for thought

For students to incorporate a new strategy into their repertoire, they must make a commitment to do so. In other words they must 'own' the strategy... students must be active participants in the teaching–learning process, and classroom discussions provide valuable opportunities for students to listen to the way others have dealt with problem-solving experiences. Open discussions are important as they allow students to evaluate strategies, consider difficulties, and explore alternative strategies that might be used in future learning activities. At the same time, teachers can listen to the way in which students talk about their learning and problem-solving, and they can facilitate the use of more effective approaches if necessary. (Ashman and Conway 1997)

The approach advocated in this book puts pupils' participation central to any intervention offered. We are trying to assist pupils to think differently about the situations they find themselves in and their responses to them. It is a cognitive change that is needed, not just a behavioural change. This same process of cognitive change applies to teacher behaviour. If both teachers and pupils can consider their responses within a transactional model framework, mutual change is more likely. Using the group work process suggested, we are also hoping that other pupils, as well as the supportive adult, will be part of the facilitating process.

Questions

How might you encourage pupils to take ownership of developing effective strategies?

How might you encourage other staff members to apply a transactional model to try to understand the cycle of responses they may be caught in?

Which staff members might be key players in implementing the approaches suggested in this book?

Pupil Action Plan

Pupil Action Plan

Name:

Tutor:

Date:

Time-scale for targets:

> **Behaviour target**
>
>
>
>
>
>
>

> **Work target**
>
>
>
>
>
>
>

> **What do I need to do to achieve my targets?**
>
>
>
>
>
>
>

How can staff help me?

Monitoring targets (discuss and sign weekly)

Date								
Initials								

Staff comments

Future action needed

Coping in Schools Scale (CISS) full version

Coping in Schools Scale (CISS)

(A structured assessment of pupils exhibiting challenging behaviour in mainstream schools)

Jane McSherry

Child's name:
Form completed by:
Date:

Instructions

To use this scale, complete each section. Score every item in every section for each child, using the following scoring system.

1. Is never able to fulfil this criterion
2. Rarely fulfils this criterion
3. More often than not fulfils this criterion
4. Almost always fulfils this criterion

Circle the number that corresponds to your assessment of the pupil on this criterion.

Please remember that this scale is part of a process. To help you with this process, each section asks for action plan suggestions. You may also wish to note other important issues under each heading.

Self Management of Behaviour

	Is never able to fulfil this criterion	Rarely fulfils this criterion	More often than not fulfils this criterion	Almost always fulfils this criterion
Can accept discipline without argument or sulking	1	2	3	4
Can cope with unstructured time, i.e. lunch and break	1	2	3	4
Can arrive and settle down quietly and appropriately	1	2	3	4
Does not leave the room without permission	1	2	3	4
Can accept changes to plans or disappointment with an even temper	1	2	3	4
Shows some self-discipline when others try to encourage deviation from normal routines at any changeover time.	1	2	3	4
Does not normally use loud exhibitionist language. Is aware of normal sound levels and can be reminded of them and respond without backchat.	1	2	3	4
Can handle trips out of school	1	2	3	4
Does not seek confrontation at break-time	1	2	3	4
Behaves appropriately in the dining hall	1	2	3	4

Score: /40

© Jane McSherry (2001) *Challenging Behaviours in Mainstream Schools*. David Fulton Publishers.

Self Management of Behaviour Action Plan

(a) Immediate

(b) Long term

Other issues to note under this heading

Self and Others

	Is never able to fulfil this criterion	Rarely fulfils this criterion	More often than not fulfils this criterion	Almost always fulfils this criterion
Can behave appropriately in the classroom	1	2	3	4
Can accept that teacher time needs to be shared	1	2	3	4
Can ask a question and *wait* for the answer and *take turns* in question and answer situations	1	2	3	4
Has appropriate communication skills: talking, asking questions, listening	1	2	3	4
Is able to work in a team	1	2	3	4
Can speak to people without resorting to rudeness	1	2	3	4
Can work in a group situation	1	2	3	4
Interacts in a positive way with peers in the playground	1	2	3	4
Can play with other children without getting 'wound up' and abusive	1	2	3	4
Can cope with large numbers of people	1	2	3	4

Score: /40

Self and Others Action Plan

(a) Immediate

(b) Long term

Other issues to note under this heading

Self Awareness

	Is never able to fulfil this criterion	Rarely fufils this criterion	More often than not fulfils this criterion	Almost always fulfils this criterion
Can ask for help	1	2	3	4
Can accept responsibility for his/her actions without employing denial/opting-out tactics	1	2	3	4
Can acknowledge own problems	1	2	3	4
Can risk failure	1	2	3	4
Is willing to accept and discuss problem areas	1	2	3	4

Score: **/20**

Self Awareness Action Plan

(a) Immediate

(b) Long term

Other issues to note under this heading

Self Confidence

	Is never able to fulfil this criterion	Rarely fufils this criterion	More often than not fulfils this criterion	Almost always fulfils this criterion
Is happy with self	1	2	3	4
Has esteem for self	1	2	3	4
Is happy with own appearance	1	2	3	4
Is happy with own hygiene	1	2	3	4

Score: /16

Self Confidence Action Plan

(a) Immediate

(b) Long term

Other issues to note under this heading

Self Organisation

	Is never able to fulfil this criterion	Rarely fulfils this criterion	More often than not fulfils this criterion	Almost always fulfils this criterion
Can work alone without constant attention	1	2	3	4
Can listen to explanations and instructions and attempts to act on advice given	1	2	3	4
Gets him/herself to school independently or, in the case of younger pupils, is willing to contemplate this	1	2	3	4
Understands the structure of lesson times within a mainstream school	1	2	3	4
Understands the teacher's role within a mainstream school	1	2	3	4
Understands the structure of places to be for lessons within a mainstream school	1	2	3	4
Understands the structure of discipline within a mainstream school – what happens if he/she is late or does not complete work, homework, etc.	1	2	3	4
Can constructively use unstructured time in the classroom	1	2	3	4
Attends regularly	1	2	3	4
Can cope in a variety of different situations	1	2	3	4
Can organise self and possessions	1	2	3	4
Can organise him/herself if help is not available	1	2	3	4
Good timekeeping, e.g. prompt arrival at lessons	1	2	3	4

Score: /52

© Jane McSherry (2001) *Challenging Behaviours in Mainstream Schools*. David Fulton Publishers.

Self Organisation Action Plan

(a) Immediate

(b) Long term

Other issues to note under this heading

Attitude

	Is never able to fulfil this criterion	Rarely fufils this criterion	More often than not fulfils this criterion	Almost always fulfils this criterion
Is prepared to work in lessons	1	2	3	4
Uses appropriate language and gestures	1	2	3	4
Wants to remain at this school	1	2	3	4
Has parental support	1	2	3	4
Wants change for themselves	1	2	3	4
Is courteous, and shows positive attitudes towards staff	1	2	3	4
Can show a positive interest in lessons	1	2	3	4
Treats school property with care	1	2	3	4
Shows a sense of humour	1	2	3	4
Goes to and stays in designated playground area	1	2	3	4

Score: /40

Attitude Action Plan

(a) Immediate

(b) Long term

Other issues to note under this heading

Learning Skills

	Is never able to fulfil this criterion	Rarely fulfils this criterion	More often than not fulfils this criterion	Almost always fulfils this criterion
Reading and numeracy up to a level that can be coped with in mainstream, given some support.	1	2	3	4
Reasonable literacy and numeracy and a willingness to improve	1	2	3	4
Has developed learning strategies to be able to use reference materials (at own level)	1	2	3	4
Has developed learning strategies to be able to ask teachers or others for advice when experiencing problems (at own level)	1	2	3	4
Does not get up and wander around	1	2	3	4
Needs a mainstream curriculum	1	2	3	4
Does not get impatient if help is not immediately forthcoming	1	2	3	4
Will try to start a task on his/her own	1	2	3	4
Is willing to try on his/her own	1	2	3	4
Generally cares about the work being done	1	2	3	4
Pays attention to class discussions and instructions	1	2	3	4

Score: /44

Learning Skills Action Plan

(a) Immediate

(b) Long term

Other issues to note under this heading

Literacy Skills

	Is never able to fulfil this criterion	Rarely fufils this criterion	More often than not fulfils this criterion	Almost always fulfils this criterion
Can read sufficiently well to read the basic instructions needed for the completion of the lessson	1	2	3	4
Is willing to spend time working out the instructions	1	2	3	4
Recognises the importance of developing reading skills even if he/she does not like reading	1	2	3	4
Will accept extra tuition on basic spelling if needed	1	2	3	4
Will recognise the need to practise spelling skills if these are weak	1	2	3	4
Can record in efficient cursive hand and is willing to practise if this is weak	1	2	3	4
Shows some appreciation of the rules of spelling	1	2	3	4
Accepts the importance of efficient dictionary skills and is willing to undertake training	1	2	3	4

Score: **/32**

© Jane McSherry (2001) *Challenging Behaviours in Mainstream Schools*. David Fulton Publishers.

Literacy Skills Action Plan

(a) Immediate

(b) Long term

Other issues to note under this heading

Score Total

Section	Score
Self Management of Behaviour	/40
Self and Others	/40
Self Awareness	/20
Self Confidence	/16
Self Organisation	/52
Attitude	/40
Learning Skills	/44
Literacy Skills	/32
Total	**/284**

Summary of Action Plans

Prioritise action plan under the following headings:

Immediate

Long term

Other issues raised

Coping in Schools Scale (CISS) (shorter version)

Coping in Schools Scale (CISS) (shorter version)

(A structured assessment of pupils exhibiting challenging behaviour in mainstream schools)

Jane McSherry

Child's name:

Form completed by:

Date:

Instructions

To use this scale, complete each section. Score every item in every section for each child, using the following scoring system.

---

1. **Is never able to fulfil this criterion**

2. **Rarely fulfils this criterion**

3. **More often than not fulfils this criterion**

4. **Almost always fulfils this criterion**

Circle the number that corresponds to your assessment of the pupil on this criterion.

Please remember that this scale is part of a process. To help you with this process, each section asks for action plan suggestions. You may also wish to note other important issues under each heading.

Self Management of Behaviour

	Is never able to fulfil this criterion	Rarely fulfils this criterion	More often than not fulfils this criterion	Almost always fulfils this criterion
Can accept discipline without argument or sulking	1	2	3	4
Can arrive and settle down quietly and appropriately	1	2	3	4
Does not leave the room without permission	1	2	3	4
Can accept changes to plans or disappointment with an even temper	1	2	3	4
Does not normally use loud exhibitionist language. Is aware of normal sound levels and can be reminded of them and respond without backchat.	1	2	3	4
Can ask for help	1	2	3	4

Score: /24

Self and Others

	Is never able to fulfil this criterion	Rarely fulfils this criterion	More often than not fulfils this criterion	Almost always fulfils this criterion
Can behave appropriately in the classroom	1	2	3	4
Can accept that teacher time needs to be shared	1	2	3	4
Can ask a question and *wait* for the answer and *take turns* in question and answer situations	1	2	3	4
Has appropriate communication skills: talking, asking questions, listening	1	2	3	4
Is able to work in a team	1	2	3	4
Can speak to people without resorting to rudeness	1	2	3	4
Can work in a group situation	1	2	3	4

Score: /28

Self Organisation

	Is never able to fulfil this criterion	Rarely fulfils this criterion	More often than not fulfils this criterion	Almost always fulfils this criterion
Can work alone without constant attention	1	2	3	4
Can listen to explanations and instructions and attempts to act on advice given	1	2	3	4
Understands the teacher's role within a mainstream school	1	2	3	4
Understands the structure of discipline within a mainstream school – what happens if he/she is late or does not complete work, homework, etc.	1	2	3	4
Can constructively use unstructured time in the classroom	1	2	3	4
Can organise self and possessions	1	2	3	4
Can organise him/herself if help is not available	1	2	3	4
Good timekeeping, e.g. prompt arrival at lessons	1	2	3	4

Score: /32

Attitude

	Is never able to fulfil this criterion	Rarely fulfils this criterion	More often than not fulfils this criterion	Almost always fulfils this criterion
Is prepared to work in lessons	1	2	3	4
Uses appropriate language and gestures	1	2	3	4
Is courteous, and shows positive attitudes towards staff	1	2	3	4
Can show a positive interest in lessons	1	2	3	4
Treats school property with care	1	2	3	4
Shows a sense of humour	1	2	3	4

Score: /24

Learning Skills

	Is never able to fulfil this criterion	Rarely fufils this criterion	More often than not fulfils this criterion	Almost always fulfils this criterion
Reading and numeracy up to a level that can be coped with in mainstream, given some support	1	2	3	4
Has developed learning strategies to be able to ask teachers or others for advice when experiencing problems (at own level)	1	2	3	4
Does not get up and wander around	1	2	3	4
Needs a mainstream curriculum	1	2	3	4
Does not get impatient if help is not immediately forthcoming	1	2	3	4
Will try to start a task on his/her own	1	2	3	4
Is willing to try on his/her own	1	2	3	4
Generally cares about the work being done	1	2	3	4
Pays attention to class discussions and instructions	1	2	3	4
Can read sufficiently well to read the basic instructions needed for the completion of the lesson	1	2	3	4
Is willing to spend time working out the instructions	1	2	3	4

Score: /44

Score Total

Section	Score
Self Management of Behaviour	/24
Self and Others	/28
Self Organisation	/32
Attitude	/24
Learning Skills	/44
Total	**/152**

Any other comments you wish to make

CISS score summary sheet

Name: Tutor Group:

CISS Full Version

Section	Self Management of Behaviour	Self and Others	Self Awareness	Self Confidence	Self Organisation	Attitude	Learning Skills	Literacy Skills	Total	%

CISS Shorter Version

Teacher/ Subject	Self Management of Behaviour	Self and Others			Self Organisation	Attitude	Learning Skills		Total	%

Range:

CISS shorter version summary sheet

Teacher Ratings Summary	Pupil Perceptions	
Name:	Tutor Group:	
Number of teachers completing the scale: 10		

Section and item	Number of teacher ratings at 1 or 2	Pupil self rating
Self Management of Behaviour		
Can accept discipline without argument or sulking		
Can arrive and settle down quietly and appropriately		
Does not leave the room without permission		
Can accept changes to plans or disappointment with an even temper		
Does not normally use loud exhibitionist language. Is aware of normal sound levels and can be reminded of them and respond without backchat		
Can ask for help		
Self and Others		
Can behave appropriately in the classroom		
Can accept teacher time needs to be shared		
Can ask a question and *wait* for the answer and *take turns* in question and answer situations		
Has appropriate communication skills: talking, asking questions, listening		
Is able to work in a team		
Can speak to people without resorting to rudeness		
Can work in a group situation		
Self Organisation		
Can work alone without constant attention		
Can listen to explanations and instructions and attempts to act on advice given		
Understands the teacher's role within a mainstream school		
Understands the structure of discipline within a mainstream school – what happens if s/he is late or does not complete work, homework, etc.		
Can constructively use unstructured time in the classroom		
Can organise self and possessions		
Can organise him/herself if help is not available		
Good timekeeping, e.g. prompt arrival at lessons		

Section and item	Number of teacher ratings at 1 or 2	Pupil self rating
Attitude		
Is prepared to work in lessons		
Uses appropriate language and gestures		
Is courteous and shows a positive towards staff		
Can show a positive interest in lessons		
Treats school property with care		
Shows a sense of humour		
Learning Skills		
Reading and numeracy up to a level that can be coped with in mainstream, given some support		
Has developed learning strategies to be able to ask teachers or others for advice when experiencing problems (at own level)		
Does not get up and wander round		
Needs a mainstream curriculum		
Does not get impatient if help is not immediately forthcoming		
Will try to start a task on his/her own		
Is willing to try on his/her own		
Generally cares about the work being done		
Pays attention to class discussions and instructions		
Can read sufficiently well to read basic instructions needed for the completion of the task		
Is willing to spend time working out the instructions		

Primary/Secondary transfer evaluation

This evaluation framework was used as the basis for discussions around the second phase of the project. It offered schools new to the project an opportunity to understand the objectives of the work and see the evidence base on which we were planning the next phase.

Evaluation of Primary Secondary Project – First Phase

Objectives of work in the first phase (Summer/Autumn 2000)

1. To assist primary schools in identifying pupils who, because of their emotional and behavioural difficulties, are at risk of failing to make a successful primary/secondary transfer
2. To gather information which enables some assessment of the child's needs
3. Preparatory intervention (limited time-scale available) for individuals and in groups
4. Communicating with receiving secondary schools about pupils' needs
5. Raising awareness of the need for relevant information exchange to take place
6. Post-transfer support to pupils and receiving staff
7. Keeping written records of interventions and evaluations

Positive outcomes detailed in the section below demonstrate that the above objectives were achieved.

Problems experienced and strategies used to overcome them

1. *Problem*
   In order to maximise money allocated it was decided to target 19 schools based on the following criteria:
   (a) schools in the Education Action Zone around one secondary school
   (b) frequent/regular uses of the Behaviour and Learning Support Service.
   A small number of schools either declined or did not respond to the invitation. The number of schools identified was too ambitious for the time available and the position in the academic year.
   Strategies
   Experience gained in the last phase has enabled more realistic planning for the second phase.
   Reducing the amount of group work offered and focusing on ensuring recorded information was useful to secondary schools to enable them to plan for incoming pupils.

2. *Problem*
   Team members were engaged in a wide diversity of other elements of their work.
   Strategies
   A need to set clear boundaries on time allocation and purpose of each piece of work.
   Put in place a system for collecting records of work.

3. *Problem*
   Schools' abilities to organise the practicalities to enable the intervention to take place.
   Strategies
   Give clearer information about what will be required for effective work to take place
   Group work intervention to take place earlier in the year, allowing a more realistic time-scale for the work to be completed

Positive outcomes

1. A cohort of appropriate pupils (with emotional and behavioural difficulties) were identified for support during transition
2. It raised the profile of these pupils' needs.
3. Some effective group work was completed in preparation for transfer.

4. Useful information was shared with schools.
5. Some secondary schools used this information directly to inform practice.
6. Feedback from pupils was that they felt supported.
7. A number of pupils are demonstrating a positive response to post-transfer support and an ability to assimilate into the secondary school culture.
8. For a small number of pupils the process highlighted significant needs that need to be targeted.
9. Primary schools targeted were very enthusiastic and positive about being involved in the project.
10. Receiving secondary schools responded very positively to the information collected and to participating in group work support.
11. A number of secondary schools committed staff resources to running post-transfer support.
12. It has raised staff awareness of the transfer needs of pupils with emotional and behavioural difficulties and encouraged debate about appropriate responses.
13. It encouraged some joined-up thinking among services in the LEA as to how we identify and respond to this cohort of pupils.

Action plan for further work

Objectives for second phase (2000–2001)
(Objectives 1–7 of Summer/Autumn 2000 input are still appropriate)

1. To redefine the schools to be targeted to set up a manageable piece of work. The criteria used for this second phase were:
   • Feeder schools in the School A Education Action Zone – this includes a number of schools that are regular and frequent users of the primary Behaviour and Learning Support service and offered support to School A in planning for the next year's intake.
   • Feeder schools into School B where inclusive practices are well established and can be further developed and used as exemplars for the LEA. This cohort also targets a number of schools that are regular and frequent users of the primary Behaviour and Learning Support service.
2. Clarify staff deployments in order to balance other priorities and to streamline the support offered to both primary and secondary schools.
3. Discuss and devise a document which outlines a menu of support on offer pre- and post-transfer.
4. Planning for the whole academic year so that support is well timed and links with pupils' secondary school visits can be made.
5. Gather, record and communicate information around identified pupils' needs.
6. Assist secondary schools in planning to meet identified needs.

Intended outcomes

1. Pupils at risk have been identified and schools plan appropriately to meet their needs, this includes:
   • Assisting primary schools in developing their systems for identifying pupils at risk at the transfer from primary to secondary school.
   • Enabling secondary schools to develop their strategies for meeting identified needs.
2. Exclusions are reduced in line with local and national targets.
3. A more inclusive educational culture is promoted across the LEA.
4. More comprehensive and informative records on pupils are exchanged and maintained which should result in more effective educational outcomes.
5. Develop more effective links between feeder primary and receiving secondary schools, resulting in more appropriate planning for pupils.

Primary/Secondary transfer pro-forma

Pupil's name:	DOB:
Parents name:	
CLA: Yes/No	CP Register: Yes/No
Feeder Primary School:	
Secondary School:	LEA:
Code of Practice Stage: 1 2 3 4 5	
Child's needs, e.g. learning, behaviour:	
Registered disabled: Yes/No	Type of disability:
Gender: M/F	Ethnicity:

The aim of this project is to offer some transfer preparation and follow up for **pupils who are identified** by their feeder primary school as being vulnerable at the transfer stage **because of their emotional and behavioural difficulties.**

Aims of the intervention:

- Raise the profile of pupils who may have difficulty with the transfer because of their emotional and behavioural difficulties.
- Data gathering to inform preparation.
- Planning for the needs of these pupils both pre- and post-transfer.
- Linking with key staff in each of the secondary schools.
- Pre-transfer preparation.
- Post-transfer support.

This booklet has been designed to give you some information about the individual pupil named above who has been part of the project. Included are scores from the Coping in Schools Scale (CISS) (McSherry 2001) which was completed by both staff and pupils; targets that .... has set and a summary of how these have been going; information from the group leader about how .... participated in the group sessions. **We include a brief summary of the key concerns and areas where you may need to offer support** for this pupil, which were derived from whole-team discussion about this pupil's needs. We hope this will be a useful tool for you in your planning and we welcome any comments or feedback.

Coping In Schools Scale – Summary Table

	SM	S&O	SA	SC	SOr	Att	LS	Lit	Total	%
Pupil										
Class										
Teacher										
Other										

Key:				
	SM	Self Management of Behaviour	**S&O**	Self and Others
	SA	Self Awareness	**SC**	Self confidence
	SOr	Self Organisation	**Att**	Attitude
	LS	Learning Skills	**Lit**	Literacy Skills

Pupil's Targets – Summary information

Pupil's Targets

1.

2.

3.

Number of weeks working on these targets:

Progress on targets:

How targets were monitored:

Who monitored the targets:

How pupil responded to the target setting process:

Group work – Summary record

Session One

SessionTwo

Session Three

Action Plan for Secondary Transfer
Key concerns and suggested areas for support

1.

2.

3.

4.

School strategies used:

Parental involvement:

Role of other agencies (past and present)

Educational Welfare:

Educational Psychologist:

Social Services:

Child and Adolescent Mental Health:

Other (please specify):

Pastoral Support Programme – meeting pro-forma

Pastoral Support Programme

Pupil's name: DOB: Year Group:

Date of meeting:

Those present   Designation

Areas of concern

Number and length of fixed-term exclusions

Reason for exclusions

Long-term behavioural objectives

Pupil input

What in-school behaviour strategies have been used?

What outside agencies have been involved?

Coping In Schools Scale (CISS) scores

	SM	S&O	SA	SConf	SO	A	LS	Lit S	Total	%
YCC										
Tutor										
Subject 1										
2										
3										
4										
5										

Review of progress on current IEP

New or amended targets (Pupil action for monitoring)

1.

2.

Further action required/people involved

Key person monitoring the PSP

Criteria for success (how will we know the targets have been achieved?)

Date of review:

Outcome of review – what is the next step?

Re-integration checklist

(This list will never be definitive because as experience is gained of re-integrating pupils and the problems those individuals have experienced there will continually be additions to the list. A consolation when things go wrong is to remember that an unforeseen hitch in one situation can lead to better planning in the next.)

Has someone from the school, e.g. tutor or learning mentor, phoned the parents/carers?

Has the pupil met with the Head of Year and tutor (secondary) or class teacher (primary) prior to starting?

Has the pupil been given a timetable and diary (secondary)?

Have any responsible peers been identified to look after the pupil during the initial stages of the re-integration?

Who is the key supportive adult for that pupil, e.g. tutor/learning mentor (secondary), class teacher/learning mentor (primary)?

Who has overall responsibility for the pupil, e.g. member of senior management/SENCO?

Where/to whom should the pupil go if they are in trouble or distressed?

Who do they need to inform if they need to leave the site (secondary)?

Where is the information on this pupil kept?

Have class teacher(s) been notified of the pupil's fears and anxieties and are they aware of any particular triggers for behaviour?

Is every member of the Senior Management Team aware of the circumstances of this pupil?

Is it appropriate for the pupil to be withdrawn from any lessons?

Who has responsibility for monitoring the overall progress of the pupil?

Have successful strategies been made explicit and shared?

For pupils who are dual registered

Are all teaching staff aware of when the pupil is expected to be off site?

Who is the contact person at the PRU?

Is there a plan to re-integrate the pupil fully when the period of dual registration comes to an end?

References

Armstrong, F., Armstrong, D. and Barton, L. (eds) (2000) *Inclusive Education: Policy, Contexts and Comparative Perspectives*. London: David Fulton Publishers.

Ashman, A. F. and Conway, R. N. F. (1997) *An Introduction to Cognitive Education: Theory and Applications*. London: Routledge.

Bentley, T. (1998) *Learning Beyond the Classroom: Education for a Changing World*. London: Routledge/Falmer.

Booth, T. (2000) 'Inclusion and exclusion policy in England: who controls the agenda', in Armstrong, F. Armstrong, D. and Barton, L. (eds) *Inclusive Education: Policy, Contexts and Comparative perspectives*. London: David Fulton Publishers.

Cooper, P., Smith, C. J. and Upton, G. (1994) *Emotional and Behavioual Difficulties: Theory to Practice*. London: Routledge.

Corbett, J. (1995) *Bad Mouthing: The Language of Special Educational Needs*. London: Taylor and Francis.

Daniels, H. *et al.* (1998) *Emotional and Behavioural Difficulties in Mainstream Schools* (DfEE Research Report RR90). London: HMSO.

Decker, S. *et al.* (eds) (1999) *Taking Children Seriously: Applications of Counselling and Therapy in Education*. London: Cassell.

DFE (1994a) *Code of Practice on the Identification of Special Educational Needs*. London: The Stationery Office.

DFE (1994b) *The Education of Children with Emotional and Behavioural Difficulties* (Circular 9/94). London: The Stationery Office.

DfEE (1999a) *Excellence in Cities*. London: The Stationery Office.

DfEE (1999b) *Social Inclusion: Pupil Support* (Circular 10/99). London: The Stationery Office.

DfEE (1999c) *Social Inclusion: the LEA role in Pupil Support* (Circular 11/99). London: The Stationery Office.

Dwivedi (ed.) (1993) *Group Work with Children and Adolescence: A Handbook*. London and Philadelphia: Jessica Kingsley.

Hallam, S. and Castle, F. (1999) *Evaluation of the Behaviour and Discipline Pilot Projects (1996–99) Supported under the Standards Fund Programme*. (DfEE Research Report RR163). London: HMSO.

INCLUDE (2000) *This Time I'll Stay: Re-integrating Young People Permanently Excluded from School: Approaches to Effective Practice from Schools and Local Education Authorities*. Ely: INCLUDE.

Jackson, S. (2000) 'Promoting the educational achievement of looked-after children', in Cox, T. (ed.) *Combating Educational Disadvantage: Meeting the Needs of Vulnerable Children*. London: Falmer Press.

Kinder *et al.* (2000) *Working Out Well: Effective Provision for Excluded Pupils*. Slough: NFER.

Maras, P. and Hall, C. (1996) *Children and Young People with EBDs: Towards a Preventative Service in Kent*. London: University of Greenwich.

McSherry, J. (1996) *A Re-integration Programme for Pupils with Emotional and Behavioural Difficuties*. London: SENJIT, Institute of Education, University of London.

Molnar, A. and Lindquist, B. (1989) *Changing Problem Behavior in Schools*. San Francisco: Jossey-Bass.

O'Brien, T. (1998) *Promoting Positive Behaviour*. London: David Fulton Publishers.

Pellegrini, A. D. and Blatchford, P. (2000) *The Child at School: Interactions with Peers and Teachers*. London: Arnold.

Rowling, J. K. (2000) *Harry Potter and the Goblet of Fire*. London: Bloomsbury.

Sameroff, A. J. (1987) 'The social context of development', in Eisenberg, N. (ed.) *Contemporary Topics in Developmental Psychology*. New York: Wiley.

Watkins, C. and Wagner, P. (2000) *Improving School Behaviour*. London: Paul Chapman Publishing.

Index